THE INTEGRITY CURE
STORIES OF A BIPOLAR HALF-LIFE

DONELLE MCKINLEY

THORNDON PRESS

This edition published in 2025 by Thorndon Press
Wellington, New Zealand

donellemckinley.com

Copyright © Donelle McKinley 2025
All rights reserved.

'Selfish' was first published in the anthology *Otherhood* by Massey University Press in 2024.

Cover designed by Donelle McKinley
Author photo by Jessica Priddy
Illustration by Yevheniia Lytvynovych
sketched-graphics.com

ISBN Paperback: 978-0-473-73605-7
ISBN ePub: 978-0-473-73606-4
ISBN Kindle: 978-0-473-73607-1
ISBN Audiobook – digital: 978-0-473-73608-8

A catalogue record for this book is available from the National Library of New Zealand.

PRAISE FOR THE INTEGRITY CURE

'A radiant, razor-sharp tour de force, *The Integrity Cure* is a remarkable memoir and a standout in mental health literature. Elegantly crafted for effortless reading, and grounded by a powerful, singular voice, it moves seamlessly between the quotidian and the sublime. Sharing fearless self-examination and poetic insight, the author offers deep companionship to all who struggle with mental illness, and lights a transformative path that serves as a mental health game changer and gateway to an exciting future. *The Integrity Cure* gives readers hope that by revealing and embracing their authentic self through honesty, they can find their way to wholeness and freedom.'

— DYANE HARWOOD, AUTHOR OF *BIRTH OF A NEW BRAIN*

'Bold, experimental, brilliant'

— DOROTHY HERSON, AUTHOR OF *THE RAG DOLL CONTRACT*

'Beautiful prose taking you on the journey of real human suffering and recovery'

— DANIEL MUNRO, AUTHOR OF *THE NAKED TRUTH*

The whole difficulty in life is to find the way between extremes — to preserve one's poise ... to get a hold of the pendulum.

Letter from Katherine Mansfield to Ida Baker
24 December 1922

CONTENTS

WILDERNESS
Both	3
The Intervention	7
The Performance	13
Under the Volcano	21
Dancing on The Bund	28
Rogue	35

BASE CAMP
Blessing	45
Selfish	48
Transported	54
Haunted	61
Flourish	65
Reading Aloud	83
Writing Lessons	88
Pivot	91

BAD WEATHER
Blank Canvas	119
Heritage	125
This Means War	136
The Baby and the Bathwater	143
Fake Grass	147
That Explains a Lot	153

ACCLIMATIZE
All That Matters	163
Typical	167
Tolerance	171
Joy is Not Negotiable	179
25 December	182

Résumé Revised	190
Instructions for Bipolar	197

SUMMIT BID

Standard Treatment	209
The Integrity Cure	216
Tuning In	221
Acknowledgments	225
About the Author	226

WILDERNESS

BOTH

In love. To fall. To love, so quick, easy, and often. To fall, to drop, to break. So many loves, so much falling, and sometimes, too many, too much, at once.

For a long time there were two of you — not only two, but always you — two sides of a yo-yo in which I grooved, spinning us high and dropping fast, breaking us over and over.

It started with a memory that flashed behind my eyes as I stood at the foot of the stairs looking up at you, seemingly for the first time. A tiny, explosive, childhood memory — the disgust of gobbling a grape that turned out to be an olive, as I stood in that same spot — marked the moment as a return, a continuation.

You were welcoming me to your home as a stranger, but we had been born in the same hospital only hours apart, our mothers becoming friends as they rested side by side. Looking back, it was as if we had a right to love; how could you be the disruptor, if you had known me first? I climbed to the top of the staircase, and followed you through the door, past the seventies kitchen, into a boisterous swirl of Seattle grunge, beer binging and laddish noise, where he was waiting for me.

He, the tallest, cockiest, most beloved alpha male of the boy-school pack, given to occasional cross-dressing in kinky nurse costumes at parties for a laugh. In a group of potentially interesting characters he was, perhaps, the least interesting, but the most relaxed and self-assured, drawing fans with his bare legs spread laid-back slouch, his certainty of mainstream success, smiling freckled wide and laughing warm as the light from the kitchen caught cheeky hints of ginger in the brown of his tight angelic curls.

You would prove to be everything he wasn't. Moody, unpredictable, and slightly insecure in a bloke's world. Your beauty was of a different place and time: olive skin, dark hair to shoulders, streaks of art class paint forgotten on the underside of your arm. Your exotic profile would bow, elbow on denimed knee, chin on palm, to consider the nuance of creative ambitions. You did not tower over me, so I could meet your eye and kiss you with the full force of two feet firmly planted. You were everything he wasn't, and I loved you both, instantly.

In our youth and immaturity, our conservative culture, our too often drunken stupid states, we had no method to navigate this chamber of mirrors with grace. That I reflected both of you, and we were all drawn to each other, was a wicked problem to wrangle instead of new territory to explore. Liberated from convention, perhaps we could have spent those years enjoying the best of each other, instead of fighting over a blanket that ultimately left everyone cold.

Imagine inverting the negative, flooding the film with light. Imagine that when I left with him that night, I told him the story of the grape and the olive and the spark that lit up your stairwell. As I lay in his bed entwined, I posed the question of you, planted the possibility of more space in which to love and be loved, and he was relaxed, self-assured, and curious. That we spoke of you without anger or fear, and when I next saw you, there was nothing to hide.

Imagine, that when I next caught your eye across a raucous, heaving room it was not with an illicit glance, but an open invitation. I could quietly excuse myself from his company with a gentle kiss untinged by a guilty lie, and slip out sideways from the crush of his audience, freeing myself into the space between. Weaving my way around the exuberant tangle of an impromptu dance floor, I joined you at the end of the bar, where we lingered cool for a while, busying hands with Camel cigarettes and adjusting to the shift in energy.

This was our local: a grand, nineteenth-century weatherboard house backing onto the rise of an inner-city park, now a university social club commandeered by undergraduates between front-loading house parties and the blur of late-night clubs. I preferred it during the day, when I could sink into the convivial lunchtime hum, the company of one person at a time, the soft arcs of sash windows, and the luxurious space of high-ceilinged rooms. On nights like this, entering under the stately portico and trailing my fingers up the long banister to the low-lit thump and rave upstairs, all elegance was forgotten.

On nights like this, I dressed like a challenge, an alter ego, bare thighed in knee-high boots, as if raising the bar for my anti-social self to strut the stage in someone else's play. I admired the apparent carelessness of your understated uniform: a carousel of t-shirts and low-slung jeans, leather band at your wrist, silver chain at your hip. The boldness of my profile drew attention, and your response, it seemed, was conflicted.

As I bantered gratefully in the easy company of your friends, and attuned to your minor-key vibe, you were sizing me up. I had made a move, but the rules of engagement were not yet clear. Until we could disappear to find our way forward, we could only stand close enough to touch, electrified and exhilarated.

When others' talk of moving on down the hill reshuffled the deck and created a diversion, I brushed your hand, locked my gaze, and silently proposed an alternative. Your answer drew us through the door, down the stairs, out onto the street, and into a waiting taxi, and in this way we bypassed an extended campaign of tortuous want.

When would I have explained that in leaving with you, I was not leaving him? Would I have waited until we were wrapped up tight in the private dark of your basement room? Before or after we lost hours to the transcendence of kiss? How would I have convinced you that it would be better this way, with room for more than one? Could I have shown you the future?

I could have raised my hand to your window in the hour before dawn, and charted a hopeful path of stars, my fingertips leaking silver ink in my desperation for you to see. A path of love without jealousy, a way to protect and evolve friendship, sustain reality instead of rumour. But what if you couldn't see?

I could have traced a different, more prophetic path, a series of ragged webs between the constellations, illuminating the years it would take us to ride out our frustration, confusion, and mistrust. Would you have believed me then?

No. You would have asked the impossible, forced me to choose. You would have whiplashed me defiantly with your tongue seven times over, until I caught a fit of giggles and begged for mercy. And so it began.

THE INTERVENTION

The first time I broke us was the eve of my baptism. A heart-pounding, eleventh-hour phone call from a number you did not recognise, a left-field monologue about cutting ties, clean slate, chastity, commitment to God. In the breaths between my declarations you begged for a middle way that I could not see, more time to talk, which I could not give. I put down the phone, walked down to the beach with my new brothers and sisters, and into the sea to be reborn.

You could not compete with a relationship that had begun at the age of four, as I sat cross-legged, straight-backed, and all attention on blessed kauri floorboards. Romantic love was no match for foundations laid in the humble Presbyterian church on the corner, a sanctuary of white weatherboard that perched on the rise, overlooking a white sand sweep of Pacific Ocean.

Back then, church meant Sunday School, and that meant stories, history, language, learning — an easy sell for a child like me. I attended until I was too old to continue, shuffling quietly up the aisle with the local children before the weekly sermon, slipping out the side door and ducking under the pohutukawa tree to the small hall for our lesson. I had never told you about that.

Your urgent appeals paled in comparison to those enshrined in my first bible, the words of Christ an enduring source of fascination and alarm in blazing red ink. My King James version, purchased on a family visit to Westminster Abbey, was a visual and tactile delight: India paper edged sky blue, corners rounded smooth, illustrated satin boards that flexed gently in my small hands. It was book as object that drew me into dense columns of grand and grown-up language at the age of six.

I had navigated the years before we met with a different bible, a hefty, serious, all-business, no-beauty textbook that looked like every other around the circle at weekly bible study. Our Baptist Church worked the New International Version hard, its contemporary language lifting us up and putting us in our place, our highlighted passages serving private inspiration, youth group discipline, and loophole interpretations.

We were a gang of untypical teenagers with our own brand of rebellion. Sneaking up the stairs to the small sound room at the back of the church, we would gossip and flirt just out of sight as the sermon played out beyond a thick shield of glass. When too much laughter gave us away, we atoned by leading worship from the stage, our music accompanying a sea of people with arms raised, voices lifted high.

Our unlovely barn of a church was situated back from the beach, a victim of continuous renovation to accommodate a growing congregation as the North Shore sprouted suburbs that merged and sprawled. Sunday packed the pews with large, conservative Christian families that flanked me when my own was falling apart. Your long-serving, spiritually-upright predecessor was the son of parents who — pillars of the church community — insisted we keep his bedroom door open at all times.

You met me on the turn, throwing the windows open for fresh air, an earnest, frustrated sixteen-year-old, subconsciously reeling from paternal abandonment and burning with big questions. For a time, we seemed to be the answer. You offered mainstream, simplicity, sex. Embraced by your secular family and tribe of friends, our relationship cleared the high bar from school to university, but in the face of evangelism dangling on the hook of an old friend, we didn't stand a chance.

The building that housed the Church of Christ was so cavernous and unremarkable, and the forces within it so intense, that its physical presence barely registered at all. For the first time, I understood that the Pentecostal congregation *was* the church, a devout spiritual family closely monitored by enigmatic leadership and a clutch of unfamiliar rules that I would learn, question, and systematically reject, one by one.

My unplanned mission to subvert began almost instantly, when, freshly baptised, I fell in love at first sight with a fellow new recruit, adding insult to your injury. Standing two rows ahead in a white V-neck t-shirt, he was singing *a cappella* along with the rest of us, his wiry, tattooed, denim-hipped frame appearing curiously out of place. When introductions followed, and he, equally drawn, skipped the small talk and doubled down on his musician cool with probing, personal questions in a soft English accent, any notions of chastity, brotherly love, were done for.

The months that you lost sight of me were a wrestle for the soul, a bizarre dance of public evangelism and private ecstasy. While you, mystified by my vanishing act, were downing cheap pints in the University Club after lectures, I was only a few blocks away in the centre of town, pep-talked and drunk on the Book of Isaiah, spiritually arm-twisted into saving the souls of strangers on Queen Street.

I was shoulder tapping people on the bus, in an effort to save them before I got off at my stop, for illicit weekends in his rented room above a garage, high on passion and poetry. In the guise of study, we took turns to read aloud naked from books on our shared undergraduate reading list, "The Sunne Rising" by John Donne forever bound to memories of a pummelled, unmade bed beneath a window on the dodgy side of town.

Sleep was optional. Run ragged by my own competing demands, I was soon alienating family and friends, and losing my grip. A consistently high achiever with plans to teach, I was suddenly skipping class and handing in sub-standard assignments. A usually reliable employee with a fierce work ethic, I was taking advantage of my autonomy and being rightfully scolded by my employer.

My faith was floundering, buffeted by extremes, and undermined by a church code of conduct that could not withstand my fierce interrogation and insistence on transparency. Refusing to accept unsubstantiated claims that leadership could be trusted with guiding my spiritual path, I demanded biblical evidence to support every suspicious rule of engagement, and quickly gained a reputation for being a troublemaker. Eventually, in a state of tear-sodden spiritual despair, I questioned my way out of faith in God altogether. At the tipping point of chaos, we proposed to drop out of university, marry, and return to England.

I'm not sure if the success of The Intervention was mostly due to the impact of my estranged parents joining forces, or the unexpected threat of being financially cut off. With one foot in adulthood, and every intention of independence, I wasn't clear what being "cut off" from middle-class parents would actually entail at that point, but my substantial consumption of Edwardian fiction had no doubt imbued the phrase with more power than it warranted.

When, a few days earlier, I had casually informed my mother that I was engaged, she laughed with apparent disdain. Ten years later, she would do this again for the same reason. Both times it felt like a cruel and unusual response, but it can't have been easy to know how to react. Somehow, as a student with no more than pocket money to my name, I was attempting to organise six bridesmaids for a full-blown, imminent wedding to someone I had recently met, with only hazy notions of life beyond it. She was not alone in her concern; the word "crazy" had begun to hum as rumours circulated among my peers.

The tag-team panel of parents was a circuit breaker for the first of many episodes that we could not name. Obscured by the follies of youth and an "artistic" temperament, all the symptoms of Bipolar Disorder Type II were there at 18, but as I sat down to face them, and for the next 28 years to come, all we knew was that I was just being me. A classic cocktail of powerful emotions — grief and love — had me rebounding from despair to hypomania, propelling me to flight. Triggered by emotional overwhelm, I was overtaken by black and white thinking, and unfounded confidence in the way forward. Desperate for a sense of control, I was convinced of the necessity to act on my impulses without delay.

I was being blindly bound to an insidious pattern that would take me nearly three decades to question: extreme moods and obsessive focus that spark rapid life decision-making, grand planning at high speed, determination to abandon a considered path, a home, people I value, in order to take a running leap into a shiny new way of being. Thinking faster than I can process, and compelled to over-share, I have no mental capacity for alternative perspectives or advice. In the absence of effective intervention, I'm further destabilised by the follow through and fall out, and primed to crash headlong into a wall of depression that can take months to recover from. Despite my resistance and resentment that day, the concern of my parents, their refusal to enable, and the formality of their planned approach, was powerful enough to grind my screaming gears to a halt.

I summoned my fiancé to the centre of town late one night: a quiet, nondescript cafe near the bus stop that I had never frequented before and would never set foot in again. As I set down his grandmother's ring on the grimy table, I numbly delivered the merciless, dictated announcement that we were over. He tried to fight for us, but I wasn't there.

The gut-wrench that followed the thawing of emotional paralysis was replaced by inconceivable shock six months later, when I received an invitation to his wedding. Another "sister" in the Church of Christ, she was the chaperone who had turned a blind eye, and the opportunist who had taken my place. Had I been drawn to a similarly vulnerable soul, or into a hidden agenda? Defeated, lost, and emotionally exhausted, I picked up the phone and called you back.

THE PERFORMANCE

ACT THREE, SCENE ONE

As Shakespeare's Rosalind strides onto the stage disguised as Ganymede, visibly liberated from design constraints and reshaped masculine, courageous, more beautiful, Ava almost lurches in her seat. Her reaction is predictable but thrilling every time: any hint of androgyny and she is drawn, captivated, liquified. With cheeks flushing in the merciful dark of the tiny Globe theatre, she crosses her legs to enable a heated squirm of longing. She is almost 50 years old; it tires and pleases her in equal measure to think that she may never grow out of this — desire, decision, as you like it.

Rosalind as Ganymede is arranging a cottage in the forest, where she can live in exile with her dear Celia until the world is put to rights in Act Five. In her mind's eye, Ava conjures a home for them on the shoestring stage almost entirely bare of props, as she has done many times over. Her imagination is charged with memory: she is young, the age of Ganymede, her wilderness a green patchwork of Stratford, Shottery, Charlecote, Wilmcote — remnants of the Forest of Arden.

On this cool autumn night, on the other side of the globe, Ava imagines an English glade in spring. She erects wooden beams, thatches a roof, plasters the walls white, affixes a door and paints it green. She positions leadlight windows at head height, and plants scented roses beneath. She places two wooden chairs inside by the fire, and makes up an iron bedstead in the other room.

ACT ONE, SCENE ONE

On the outskirts of Stratford upon Avon, 22-year-old Ava is sitting on a wooden chair in the middle of the kitchen, sheared handfuls of chestnut hair on the lino at her feet. Her stillness masks the wild hammering in her chest; only the remains of dinner on the table betray the spontaneity of the act. Her blond bombshell of a flatmate hovers in front of her, considering her handiwork, their orange all-purpose scissors swinging from her polished index finger.

"Enough?"

Ava feels her head with her hands.

"Maybe a bit shorter all over."

"Do you want to look in the mirror?"

"Nope."

"Are you *sure*?"

"Yep."

Audrey grins, and reaches for her glass of wine. Actress. Enabler. Always up for a lark. If anyone could appreciate a mistress of reinvention, it's Audrey. Last year, she asked Ava to take photos of her posing in their bathroom, wrapped in a white towel and pouting at the camera like Marilyn Monroe. Not Ava's type at all.

Unlike Audrey, who finds her own vanity amusing, Ava doesn't much care what she looks like, only that she looks different, right now. Her misery has become unbearable, and she is desperate for some relief. Perhaps, if she looks less like the woman *he* wants, and more like the woman *she* wants, she can find a way to unhitch herself from the self-inflicted, long-distance, long-term trajectory that is causing her so much distress. As far as Audrey is concerned though, the haircut is just a light-hearted whim after one glass too many on a Friday night. Audrey has heard the sobbing from the bedroom down the hall, but Ava doesn't want to get into it; framing her request as a dare is the easiest way to get her flatmate to play along.

Audrey pauses behind her, nods Ava's head towards her chest a fraction.

"Olivia's coming for dinner on Sunday. Will you be here?"

Ava's cheeks flush hot as she fidgets in her chair.

"Yep."

ACT ONE, SCENE TWO

Olivia is lying so still and so separate in Ava's king-size bed that Ava feels like she's going to burst at the seams with longing. It is New Year's Eve, or technically, New Year's Day, and she is drunk. Too drunk to feel the cold, too drunk to stop the ceiling from spinning, but not drunk enough to risk outright rejection.

They have been working alongside one another as chefs for weeks, but Olivia still feels like Audrey's Friend before Ava's. Friendship/flatmate protocol in all its vagueness has never been as frustrating as it is right now, at the very moment when all hell should be breaking loose in the best possible way.

Between Ava's inexperience and Olivia's natural reserve, a drunken night out had seemed a crude but necessary opportunity to release the flirty undercurrent of their nightly dance around blazing gas rings, cauldrons of stock, and heavy cast iron saucepans oozing butter. Outside the steaming, frantic kitchen, with aprons off and nothing to distract them from each other, politeness and shyness has been confusing the signals and weighing them down like swimmers in overcoats.

In the next room, Audrey's inebriated snores have declared it safe to proceed. Drunken laughter beneath Ava's window breaks the silence on Scholars Lane, but neither uses it as an excuse to speak or move. Perhaps Olivia really is asleep, but Ava is too paralysed by fear and desire to whisper the question. Why, frets Ava, does she always feel compelled to initiate, and why must she always try to play by the rules even when she's not sure what they are? They are wasting time. If Ava's going to divert from The Plan, it needs to happen soon.

ACT TWO, SCENE ONE

A flurried, sleep-deprived, suitcase of nerves, Ava rushes to the gate and scans the stream of people coming through international arrivals. The bus from Stratford to Heathrow airport tossed her out at the crack of dawn, and the crease-free advantage of her new polyester shirt has been trounced by the trapped stench of anxious sweat. She wishes there was time to shower and change, but suddenly he is there, surprising her from an unexpected direction, and clearly annoyed to have been kept waiting after a long-haul flight. He hasn't changed a bit.

Before Ava can form a coherent sentence, he is looking her up and down with absolute horror: his girlfriend is barely recognisable. Since the last time she sent him a photo, Ava's glossy shoulder-length hair has been hacked into a messy pixie cut, and her Pacific Ocean tan has paled to landlocked grey. The athletic figure he last embraced has morphed to strain wide-waisted trousers, and her signature ballet flats have been replaced by workman's leather boots. He requires Ava's pathetic prompt to kiss, and delivers it cold, confused, perfunctorily.

Sensing impending disaster, Ava is too beside herself to do anything but stick helplessly to her plan for a perfect reunion. She guides the way through the crowd to the baggage carousel, and down to the tube for North London. She has chosen a quiet, affordable place where she imagines they will fuck, sleep, talk, and set their relationship to rights by the next morning. The inconvenient questions of who and what she is now, who and what she wants, have been relegated to the too-hard file in the pit of her stomach, where she hopes they will dissolve overnight.

After a year apart, with only scant communication bridging the gap, the intensity of being in the same place at the same time is overwhelming, the awkwardness of communication excruciating. As they sit side by side, backpacks at their feet, eyes averted, their conversation lurches like the stop-start of the train, saying little, meaning nothing, strangers out of synch.

He can't understand why they aren't going straight to their friends' flat, where they are expected the next day, forcing Ava to rehash her romantic vision of time alone together, before surrounding themselves with six boisterous friends they have known since high school. If he's wondering how the bisexuality he had accepted as an irrelevant quirk of Ava's has become something else entirely, he says nothing.

ACT TWO, SCENE TWO

Arriving at their destination after a more tiresome walk than Ava anticipated, they climb the stairs of the humble suburban bed and breakfast like a couple to the gallows. Ava, who can't regroup until liberated from her wretched, ill-chosen clothing and clammy skin, temporarily diffuses the tension by disappearing for a bath. By the time she emerges, fragile but clean, and wrapped in a mean, threadbare towel, he is reading the sports section of a newspaper on the bed. Some things haven't changed.

Overriding every instinct, Ava is convinced that sex is the only thing that will dispel the awful atmosphere, the only thing that can reconnect them and her deeply divided self; it has been, after all, the basis of their relationship. She steels herself to initiate — to rip the plaster off. She casts her mind back to easier times, when sex with each other required no thought, planning, or effort. She casts her mind forward to their future together — he is, unofficially, her husband to be — but Ava is playing by a script that no longer rings true.

She has never had to cajole before, and it's sickening for them both. Eventually, he makes a half-hearted attempt to meet her halfway, and she is mortified when, for the first time in five years, he can't perform. He begs off, muttering exhaustion, jetlag. Turning onto her back, Ava mutely releases the reigns of the day, and permits herself to sink into sadness and defeat. Since she left Olivia standing at the bus-stop in the dark, the day has felt interminable. It is 9 am.

ACT THREE, SCENE TWO

Ava discretely checks her watch in the reflected light of the stage; she never tires of Shakespeare, but it has been a long day. It is 9 pm and everything is being sorted, settled and tied up in a predictable, comedic bow. Rosalind, still disguised as Ganymede, is telling her besotted Orlando that she is a magician, she can set Rosalind before him tomorrow to be married. Declaring over and over that he loves no woman, Ganymede assures that all will be well, as long as everyone meets at the same place at the same time, and so it is. As the actors break into the dancing finale — always her favourite part — Ava pauses memory and claps along with the audience, a huge grin on her face.

As she shuffles out of the theatre into the chill of the evening, Ava doesn't want to remember what happened next. She doesn't want to remember how a young woman — the world her oyster — wasted more precious time whipping herself up into an emotional tornado, only to inevitably come crashing down. She wants so much to banish that year of her life from memory, that she almost successfully has.

She doesn't want to remember the appalling performance with her boyfriend, tripping around Europe ostensibly carefree. Her daily mood swings, between the divine highs of art and architecture, and the anguish of sexual confusion. Wretched nights crying inconsolably in the awful confinement of a two-person tent. Hysterical arguments pacing train platforms and city squares, her inability to articulate what was really going on.

She doesn't want to remember how a newly independent university graduate became so debilitated with depression that she had to fly home to live with her mother — the person who had silently declared her attraction to women unacceptable. The months of struggle, working a string of part-time jobs making coffee, scooping popcorn, and tending bar. If she must remember, it needs to be in another way. She needs a character to assert safe distance.

ACT THREE, SCENE THREE

People joke that life should come with a manual, but what if you really are a textbook case and for years you didn't have the book? When, at the age of 46, I considered a textbook checklist of cognitive distortions associated with Bipolar Type II, I experienced a misplaced rush of over-achievement as I ticked every one.

After almost 30 years of blindness, suddenly it was staring me in the face: my proneness, when emotionally overwhelmed, to think in a way that is distorted and misaligned with reality. There it was, all tidy and left-justified, the shorthand descriptors bold as brass: Catastrophizing, All-or-Nothing, Fortune Telling, Mind Reading, Should Statements. The chilling, illuminating catalogue of culprits went on, all fuelling my drastic reactions to ambiguous or harmless situations.

At the age of 46, I didn't need to read the example scenarios that illustrate how this type of thinking can play out — it had been the story of my life to date. What I needed was this list of distortions a long time ago, and some expertise and support to extract myself from their grip. Armed with this knowledge at the age of 22, I would have understood the need to pause, process, and reassess. Instead of wasting a precious year playing out a misguided script, I could have screwed up the courage to spend twenty seconds saying a few seemingly impossible things to one perfectly reasonable person before they got on a plane: *I'm sorry, things have changed. I no longer want to do what we planned. I might be gay — I'm not sure — and I need time to work it out. I love you, but I can no longer be in this relationship.*

It would have amazed me, but the world wouldn't have ended. I would have put down the receiver, stepped out of the red phone box, and walked back up the stairs to my tiny flat in Stratford Old Town. I would have collapsed in my old brown armchair and sat there stunned, or cried myself out. I might have slept, or walked the cobbled streets for hours — perhaps both.

I would have worked some restaurant shifts, seen some friends, gone to the theatre, as the relief of being able to stay put where I was content slowly set me upright. Then, after as many days as it took to find my centre, I would have sat down at my typewriter under the kitchen window, reread my last chapter, rolled in a fresh sheet of paper, and got back to work.

UNDER THE VOLCANO

On this wet Friday afternoon in spring, the bookshop is quiet but for the divine background chatter that not everyone hears. From the rare to the recent they are everywhere — authors and characters with so much to say. Floor to ceiling, wall to wall, propped in corners, stacked on tables, stashed beneath the stairs, stuffed in the mezzanine. The latest theme colouring the window, the bright popular fluff arms reach from the threshold for the non-committal. Hardback first editions in glitzy Mylar covers showing off behind the counter, leatherbound elderly swapping memories in antique glass cabinets. In this sacred space — swaddled in the printed word, soothed by story and tactile tasks — the blessed bookdealer dissolves.

The next book plucked from the box and dusted off prompts an affectionate sigh. The familiar oval line drawing tugs gently at the heart like the sinker of a child's first fishing line. Ratty and Mole are rowing the river on a late summer's night, about to disappear out of frame beneath the arched stone bridge up ahead. In a few hours they will encounter the Piper at the Gates of Dawn. The charming black and white sketch makes the 1968 reprint, in an attractive green dust wrapper, a solid contender for a humble collection. Not rare, but dear. A cosy, comfortable octavo for small hands, not too heavy to hold above your head as you lie in the shade of a tree on a summer's day.

A light sweep of the left hand across the cover (a discrete, much practised caress) before the reveal: green cloth boards held by many hands, or perhaps few, and often — proof of love. A riffle of pages from back to front decides: we can forgive the boards their edgewear, fading, and ink stains. The pages are clean, the illustrations intact, the binding sound. A moment's thought and it is done: in the soft dark scratch of a favoured 6B, a pocket-money price appears in the top right corner of the front free endpaper. Better that Ratty and Mole find a new home before collecting dust in their temporary lodgings.

The Wind in the Willows joins the pile for shelving as the heavens open again. Look up, look out, reorient. Through the open wooden door, the smell of warm roads washed clean, the hiss of after-school carloads coursing the slope of the main street from the slumbering volcano to Waitemata Harbour, the drumming of old corrugated iron above the sheltering book trolley out to tempt passersby.

Time for a stretch of the legs to the broom cupboard kitchen: up from the favoured footstool catching loose threads of sea-green carpet, a roll of stiff shoulders, an arm stretch to the sky. Five strides through Visual Arts and a corridor of Literary Fiction, three steps down from E to F where the light is dim, through the door on the right before Cooking and Self-help. A naked bulb, a teacup with roses, a spoon of Earl Grey, the forgotten but welcome remainder of an over-sized date scone. Scribbled quotes and random reflections on painted white bricks amuse while the kettle rumbles and roils.

As the tea steeps, the tired creak of Edwardian floorboards announces a customer, or in this case, a seller: two rain-spattered banana boxes with burly arms and legs and the glimpse of a balding head. Promptly unburdened, the seller is encouraged to browse but opts to hover, which makes no difference.

The assessment from the footstool is swift and satisfying, the books assigned to one of two camps: the larger Yes Please, the smaller No Thank You (we have these already / but how do you know?). On a slip of paper two prices are scribbled: cash or credit, which will it be? A ping and swoosh from the cash register, a scrawled signature in the logbook, and the shop becomes the happy way station for a medley of popular biographies, spotless cookbooks, and recent crime fiction — all perfectly ordinary but respectable bookshop fare.

Unlike the victims of a mere domestic declutter, the real treasures rarely appear unexpectedly at the door. One must formally call upon them in situ to honour and relieve the inevitable impact of emigration, downsizing, desperation or death (for nothing less will separate a bibliophile from their books).

First, the phone call, and the occasionally cool but typically urgent invitation to appraise (the awful task having been left to the last minute). Next, the polite screening questions to test the waters: how many, which subjects, how far away? Assured of a sea of paper and ink that flows from room to room, bubbles up to the attic, spills into the garage, there is no time to waste, for there are other dealers, and it is important to arrive first.

And so it is, in this way, that many fruitful hours may be spent, wading knee-deep through unchartered territory, scooping up armfuls of heritage like autumn windfall apples. In this way, an attuned dealer, who has promptly spied a first edition James Joyce on a top shelf, will be delighted but not surprised that it leads to a swathe of Woolf, a pocket of

Hemingway, a tranche of Pound, and other friends of Shakespeare & Company. The aching back, dirty knees, and filthy hands at the end of such a day is nothing compared to the magnificence of the haul.

Other phone calls lead down different paths, different obsessions: national history, military history, trains, planes and automobiles, music, science fiction, spiritualism, the occult. The largest acquisitions — unceremoniously decanted to rented shipping containers until their contents can be researched, priced, and catalogued — will likely be scattered to the winds once sold, and so the cycle of collecting begins again.

A second attempt at tea is almost disrupted by a burst of chatter like a flock of startled pigeons through the door, but it's only the beautiful, high-spirited assistant back from the post office, swapping local gossip with a retired regular walking in the same direction. What will be the fate of the long-serving antique shop next door, recently decamped in the face of rent hikes? What will replace it? Having tucked the gentleman's umbrella behind the door and reassured themselves that at least the bookshop isn't going anywhere for the foreseeable future, the assistant gathers up the pile for shelving from the carpet and heads downstairs, the regular disappears into the poetry room until closing, and the library hush resettles.

Teacup stowed behind the counter, attention returns to task. A craft knife sculpts wood and lead to a pleasing, productive point. A hand lucky dips back into the stream, catches a smooth, slim, red volume, glistening gold. *Christmas Books* by Charles Dickens, what luck at this time of year. A handsome, gift-perfect, gilt-stamped edition, decorative purple endpapers clean and proud. One of a series separated from its mates, but no matter. It is lovely, timely, and affordable. Priced and polished, red top edge dusted with a filbert paintbrush, it joins the curated cubby in front of the register until December — if it lasts that long.

Next, a handful of slender paperbacks skimmed from the surface, appraised and dispatched fondly: the ninth hazardous adventure of *The Famous Five*, *Paddington Abroad* complete with beret, *White Boots*, *Ballet Shoes*, and the curious *Borrowers*. Further down, the fourth *Harry Potter*, a decent run of Dahl, some Maurice Gee, and then it's *Rupert Bear* annuals all the way to the bottom. Ah yes, the Ruperts — one of many armloads ferried from last month's sprawling trestle table book fair. The jolly, red-jumpered bears are set aside for a scan of the bulging customer wish list, where a ready home might be waiting with open arms.

A peek at the clock ticking imperceptibly behind the counter, and there is time to tackle some curiosities before closing. A press, a click, and the unlovely machine on the wooden desk in the poky corner by the phone wakes slowly from its slumber, grunting and wheezing like a grudging old uncle from an afternoon nap. Finally, the screen lights up with the demanding glare of an international marketplace — the commoner's testing ground of choice for rarity and value.

Logging in, there is an uncomfortable shift in the atmosphere, as if the bookshop is being pulled through the online portal from sleepy Devonport into the shoving, squeezing hustle and bustle of London's Portobello Road market on a Saturday morning. How else, though, to determine how a particular copy of an unusual book compares to others of its kind, or discover, in fact, that it is not so unusual, and not worth comparing at all? How else to settle on a competitive price for a rare book that is more likely to find an owner on the other side of the world than close to home?

Today's subjects of analysis are a motley crew, the pointy

tip of a mountainous backlog in the storeroom beside the desk. Two large folios: weighty tomes bound in crumbling leather, exhausted nineteenth-century spines cracked and peeling like bark, their beautiful illustrations (all accounted for) miraculously spared from the fate of bookbreaking. Balanced atop them, a couple of tidy, maybe collectable James Bonds, wrappers intact, and a few sought-after military histories that pop up less often these days. A never-seen-before hardback first edition of a vaguely familiar author (just in case), some garish sixties paperbacks (you never know with science fiction), and a petite, sweet-scented, vellum-bound incunabula that has travelled from Europe for over five hundred years, like a message in a bottle, to wash up at the bottom of the world.

The tinkle of a piano, the faintest crackle, and the voice of Billie Holiday like warm honey, spreading through the shop. The assistant, it seems, has had enough silence for one day. Returning from downstairs, which thanks to her efforts is now ship shape, she arrives just in time to intercept the ringing phone. Having politely redirected a customer on the hunt for a VW Beetle car manual to the larger sister shop across the bridge, she starts wading through the exercise book on the counter, looking for homes for Rupert.

A violent clatter outside interrupts us both, but it's only the bright orange sandwich board knocked flat by a gust of wind. The squally weather is turning again, as it so often does, toying with the residents of the small peninsula, who never know what to wear.

A stretch of the legs to rescue the languishing sign, and a wave to the owner of the new bookshop opposite, who, like an uncanny mirror image, is doing the same thing. The lights have come on in the Italian restaurant above her, and the fish and chip shop next door; they, and a host of others, will keep the main street humming when shops like ours have turned in for the night.

Lingering on the footpath to conjure a theme for the next window (Halloween?), the secondhand bookshop casts an almost Dickensian glow. Its name — a familiar mouthful shorthanded by so many book lovers — arches across the glass in bold swirls of Christmas green, red, and gold, pinned by a court jester in the top left corner. An artful display of books on design nestles amongst the default props: a small reading lamp, a miniature rocking chair, a faded globe. It is almost as if you could shake the scene gently, and snow would fall. To stay and call this home might be a pleasant life, a predictable life, but all the stories that lie within were written from the world beyond.

DANCING ON THE BUND

A flash of colour on the other side of the glass draws Isabel's bleary gaze down from the hotel heights. For a moment, all she can see is the blur of shouting billboards, blinking signage and breakfast commuter swarm, but then there it is again: a graceful arc of red slicing the air, a giant fan, many fans — sky blue, sunshine yellow — a fan dance. An orderly, evenly spaced cluster of senior citizens in a concrete public square, their synchronised movements greeting the day as one. If there is tinny music blaring from a speaker, she cannot hear it; in her soundproofed silence the dance recalls tai chi, with its gentle shifts and sway.

Isabel has never seen people dancing outside in the morning, and this unexpected spark of joy stirs life beneath the numbness. She rises from the hard floor, where she has been sitting pretzelled by the bed, to start a long day of killing time. She showers on auto pilot in the green gloom of the budget bathroom, and rummages carelessly in her suitcase for something cool to wear. At once cabin feverish, and in no hurry to go anywhere in a place she feels under surveillance, she has thought no further than swirling out through the revolving doors of the lobby onto the streets of Shanghai.

Four hours inland, outside the window Isabel abandoned yesterday, the college rubbish dump is stinking in the rising spring heat that promises worse to come, steaming and stewing the resident waste from rooms above, below and beside. A grey ceiling of cloud squats low and heavy over the dusty tract of bare land that disappears into haze. Inside, her empty apartment rings with the persistent brown drip of the bathroom tap. The unwrapped gift of a new rice cooker in cellophane and red ribbon still stands untouched on the kitchen bench.

Downstairs, the small military-like campus is stirring around the office of the Deputy Head, who has been awake for two hours, cleaning up the administrative mess of the English language teacher who could not be persuaded to stay. Thirsty, she holds her fingers to the blue and white teapot beside her; the porcelain is cold, but she pours out the last of the tea anyway.

Weary and frustrated, the Deputy can't make sense of it. She had done everything in her power to make the new teacher welcome, and the girl had seemed so promising. At the formal reception dinner, Isabel had been respectful but confident with her new colleagues, and willing to try every unfamiliar dish that appeared on the turntable in front of her. It had been hard to know what to expect of the first native English speaker the college had employed, but the girl's basic Mandarin was sound, and she seemed eager to improve.

The following day, dismissing the girl's preference to explore alone, the Deputy Head had introduced the students assigned to show the new recruit around the city, and watched them hang on her every word. The foreigner spoke English clearly, listened to their efforts patiently, and seemed intelligent and kind — all the makings of a good teacher. So much for that.

Before classes had even begun, the girl had requested an

urgent meeting. She had sat down opposite where the Deputy Head sat now, her face flushed and tearful. She had said this wasn't the right place for her, and she needed to leave immediately. The girl's profuse apologies barely registered as the Deputy's mind began to swim with the implications for students and the reputation of the college. The inevitable phone calls from influential, angry parents. The likely impossibility of finding a replacement native speaker at short notice. The threat of this chaos to her own position. The girl had been polite but insistent — there was nothing the Deputy could say to change her mind.

None of it made sense to her, but the Deputy had to deal with it all the same. She set down her cup to give her stiff shoulders a satisfying crack, her aching neck a slow stretch from side to side, back to front. Perhaps she can take just a few minutes for breakfast before she continues. For the rest of the day, she will be juggling damage control and the urgent meetings in her over-booked schedule until she reports to the Head, due back from conference this afternoon. As she stands slowly, her middle-aged knees protesting, she glances again at the tea-stained scrap of notepaper on her desk: the name of a Shanghai hotel where the girl has reportedly checked in, the date and time of a flight to Sydney, when the deserter will no longer be her responsibility. Four days to go.

Walking west, Isabel can sense water before she sees it, and picks up the pace to give her restless legs a decent stretch. Dodging the traffic to cross over to the famous promenade, she stops to take in the curve of Huangpu River — a disappointing, muddy grey mirror of buildings and sky. To Isabel, any body of water is better than none, but the murky passage does little to shift the suffocating weight of landlock lodged in her chest.

Under better circumstances, The Bund might have been a source of fascination, with its congregation of nineteenth-century colonial architecture preaching Neo-Classical, Baroque, and Gothic, but this morning Isabel has no interest. Perhaps she would have experienced it differently as a sightseer fresh off the plane, her perception untarnished by the ugly, pollution-belching industry she has witnessed sprawling through the provinces behind her. Either way, the time and place are all wrong: she is not a tourist, she is not meant to be here. She should be miles inland, planning lessons. As guilt-ridden and aimless as a prisoner on a courtyard circuit, she walks north beneath the chain of streetlamps, taking in great gulps of air.

———

Crouching on the floor of a narrow resource cupboard, opposite the classroom assigned to Isabel, Mǐn Guo is breaking the seal of a heavy cardboard box of books that the English teacher has left behind. If Mǐn is going to be thrown in the deep end and cover classes, perhaps there is something in here that can help her. At the very least, she can satisfy her curiosity about the contents of the box, which has been sitting here since it arrived from New Zealand three weeks ago.

She unpacks in handfuls, stacking the books in tidy piles higher up on an empty shelf, where the light is better. When she reaches the bottom she stands, straightens her blouse and uses a corner to polish her glasses, before considering the books, one by one. She starts with the largest — a *Concise Oxford English Dictionary*, a *Collins Chinese Dictionary*, an English thesaurus. There are language textbooks for English and Mandarin: beginner, intermediate and advanced. Useful. A glossy China travel guide in English, and a fold-out map of the country. Less useful.

The remaining paperbacks in English appear to be novels.

Charles Dickens and Jane Austen she recognises, but other names are new to her. For the first time she sounds the names of Charlotte Brontë, E. M. Forster, Katherine Mansfield, Margaret Atwood, Jeanette Winterson, Michael Chabon. She lingers over the cover of *A Room with a View*, intrigued by the painting of a palace, or a church perhaps. Mǐn will ask permission to read these before deciding whether or not they are appropriate for teaching translation. With any luck they won't be, and she can keep them for herself.

On the other side of the campus, Píng Zhang clambers up the concrete stairs of a nondescript building with a blue bucket, mop and cleaning supplies. On the second floor landing she steps aside to let an exiting resident pass, before unlocking the door of the English teacher's apartment. She has been instructed to clean thoroughly for the next resident; the English teacher has left before term has even begun, which makes no sense at all.

A quick survey of the apartment finds little to be done since Píng was last here. Her colleagues had teased that a Westerner would make more work for her, but the English teacher has left everything so clean and tidy, it's almost as if she was never here at all. The bathroom is spotless, and the kitchen looks like it hasn't been used; the gifted supplies of rice and noodles are stacked on the bench just as they were a few days ago. There is no evidence of the teacher's wretched, restless nights; she has stripped the single mattress and piled the laundry. The furniture in the main room is just as Píng had arranged it: single bed against the back wall, wooden desk by the kitchen door, and the small low table beneath the window, but the teacher has left some things behind. A large book sits on the table, a piece of white paper is folded in half on the desk.

Píng doesn't dare to sit down and look at these properly in case someone walks in, but she wipes her hands on her apron and stoops over the table to flip through the book with forefinger and thumb. The pages are full of large colour pictures: snow-capped mountains mirrored in lakes, bright green fields dotted with sheep, huge gnarled trees with red flowers like fireworks, expensive-looking boats, lots of blue sky, sand and sea. Most of the pictures are empty of people, which makes them a bit strange to her eye, as if the places aren't quite real.

Píng lets the cover of the book drop, and walks over to the desk. She hesitates above the folded paper, which she sees now is curiously addressed to the college students in Chinese. She doesn't want to touch it, in case it's the wrong thing to do. She moves to the side of the desk, crouches down half-way, and squints to see if she can read any of the contents through the slight bounce in the fold, but all she can make out is a page of scrawl in what appears to be not-Chinese.

She will give the apartment a once over with disinfectant before she decides whether to take the book and letter with her, or simply report them to her supervisor. As she pulls on her rubber gloves, Píng tries to imagine what it would be like to have this — the best teacher apartment — all to herself. Her own space, large windows, everything as tidy as she had left it when she came home from work each evening. The silence, the luxury. Impossible.

———

The overcast sky is threatening rain, but strains of music up ahead keep Isabel moving forward until she sees them: a dozen elderly couples in everyday clothes, dancing a foxtrot in the middle of the bustling promenade. Dancing in the morning, it seems, is a custom. She admits a half-smile of delight in spite of herself, and sits down beneath a tree to watch them. There is something strange but soothing about people dancing when her world is spinning on its head.

As she lets herself sink into their slow-slow-side rhythm,

Isabel isn't thinking about the past year of intensive preparation: the investment of time, money and effort in weekly language lessons with her Chinese tutor; the stacks of library books she has devoured on Chinese history and culture; the months spent learning to break down English grammar and vocabulary into teachable chunks. She isn't thinking about the steady, determined saving for a one-way ticket and nominal emergency fund from her meagre wages, or the much-handled photos sent from the Deputy Head that had kept her motivated: lush green mountainscapes evoking traditional Chinese paintings, which she had mistakenly assumed to be her destination.

She isn't questioning the knee-cracking speed of her decision to turn her back on the opportunity that she has worked hard for. She isn't dwelling on the scorched earth of a professional life she now has to rebuild, or the multi-headed hydra of her love life, which is waiting to ensnare her on return. Her China Project is simply over, and people are dancing on The Bund. She won't be able to think clearly about anything until she feels completely free, surrounded by ocean, beneath a giant blue fan of sky.

ROGUE

He first hooks Brooklyn with the lure of books. Big, bright, glossy, as-new art and design books. High quality, coffee-table eye candy. The kind of books that would sell from her shop window within days. The kind of books she is required to ask questions about, request identification for, in case they have been stolen.

The consummate cliché of tall, dark and handsome, he is exceptionally polite, and she doesn't want to be rude. She angles: How can he part with such beautiful books? He hazily alludes to reference for his work, and says he no longer has need of them. He seems that type: the commercial design type. He exudes the relaxed confidence that Brooklyn associates with the ability to conceptualise, create, and charge a lot of money for it. He is also, she thinks, completely out of her league.

With an endearing blush, he explains his paint-spattered shorts and jandals — he has a few days off, and is helping a friend to paint his house nearby. He is not often in this part of town. When she comments on the hot weather, he says they are painting inside — surfing explains the tan. Attempts at self-deprecation are charming, but there's no denying it: the man is a god.

By the time Brooklyn has slowly assessed his stack of books

and offered a price, she has been small-talked and bantered to a crush. He says he doesn't have a driver's licence because he doesn't drive, and not wanting to press for a passport that no one carries, she waves away the formalities and logs the shop purchase under the name he offers. He becomes an occasional seller who will only deal with her, and she nicknames him Sunshine.

Two years later, after Brooklyn has moved to a sister bookshop in the heart of the city, he appears in the doorway unexpectedly one afternoon and proposes coffee. She hasn't seen him in a while, and he wears a new vulnerability — tired around the eyes, or perhaps a little haunted. Brooklyn, surprised but helpfully less intimidated, suggests the cafe a few doors down.

Slumped in a violet vinyl booth, his paleness and bewildered air cast a different light on his beauty. He has no books to sell. Is this invitation then, what she has been waiting for? He is mostly quiet and prefers to listen. Brooklyn too, is disoriented. One broken engagement, two jobs, and four house moves have upended her since they first met. An expected promotion has fallen through, and mortgage payments on her hotel apartment are becoming a struggle. She is frustrated, feeling trapped, and thinking about moving overseas — so is he.

The details of his circumstances are hazy, but it's clear that he enjoys her company. They start meeting in the city after she closes the shop for the day, drifting between cafes and talking for hours. Brooklyn loves the depths and range of his voice, the lift of tone and spirit, and the way they giggle like idiots over childhood memories and reenactments of shared popular culture. She loves that she can light him up. She accepts everything that might be considered a weakness; it puts him within her reach. Eventually, she needs to know. He gives in to her polite persistence, admits to the complication of a girlfriend, and stops dropping by.

Weeks later, when Brooklyn has impulsively quit the bookshop, sold her apartment, purchased flights, and packed her bags for a new life in Thailand, he calls to say he is in love with her. Allegedly, it's no longer complicated. Brooklyn, who did not think twice about the total life upheaval she is in the process of executing, doesn't think twice about changing direction. She can run away, or run to — either way, she is still running.

Wielding her talent to pivot at dizzying speed, Brooklyn goes on a travel cancellation spree, losing money at every turn. Within hours, she is completely boundless and free to embrace an alternative future with him. Within hours, there is a new plan: she will use her savings, for as long as they hold out, to do nothing but write.

She rents a one-bedroom apartment that becomes the almost unchanging backdrop to their relationship. He rarely wants to meet anywhere else. Having sold almost all her possessions before her intended international departure, Brooklyn's rooms are sparsely furnished. A small, cream, antique sofa commands the centre of the living room, a secondhand side table for her typewriter and low wooden chair attend the window. A handful of framed Art Deco prints on the walls, stacks of books on the floor. The bedroom is a burgundy-wrapped double bed, mirrored in an elaborate gilded oval.

The heritage-listed building smells of overcooked beef and boiled cabbage, and has seen better days. The real prize is the elegant facade of 1930s red brick framed in white stone, and the generous light from six stories of green-trimmed sash windows. The old-New York forest green arch, and black and white tiled entrance. Wide wooden doors and a staircase sweeping worn red carpet up to her rooms on the fifth floor. The building sits on an attractive rise with a peek of the harbour, between main street and university, a short walk to art galleries and the park. Brooklyn has always prioritised prime location and beauty over budget.

She spends her mornings crafting poetry, and afternoons at the library or the dance studio around the corner. They ease into languid, luxurious evenings in her apartment, arm's reach from lazy Thai takeaway or decadent feasts of oysters and champagne, swapping the highlights of their day. Sworn to confidentiality by the high-profile creative company he works for, his tales are brief and trivial. Brooklyn is all too willing to be distracted from conversation; together, they excel at sex — equally bold and willing to yield.

After a few weeks of heady honeymooning, he is contracted to work with a renowned film company, which requires employees to leave their phones at reception until the end of the day. He commutes cross-country and works long hours, intensifying their time together, which he doesn't want to waste on meeting family and friends. There is light-hearted talk of marriage.

When her savings dwindle, Brooklyn starts working for a multi-national publisher. The job involves frequent travel, and to his frustration, she too becomes less available. There is one glorious, debaucherous weekend at his uninhabited childhood home on the coast a few hours south, but mostly they exist for one another in text messages and late-night phone calls.

Always quick to perfect imperfection, Brooklyn proposes they set up a new base together — somewhere larger, slicker, more *him* — to simplify logistics. She suggests a newly renovated apartment in the heritage hotel she has called home before, which is surely worth the small fortune in rent.

The property agent pushes application forms across the desk for each of them, and sits back to wait. Excited, Brooklyn moves quickly through the mandatory lines and squares, but can't help noticing that he is slow to do so. His page is angled away from her, his left arm propped for privacy. The formal identification they are required to provide is obscured by his palm. Palpably tense, he completes the form in silence, and slides it back across the table face down. He fumbles with the awkward question of the rental deposit to be split, which she waves away and pays.

After weeks of infuriating vagueness and little contact, his strange behaviour, and apparent reluctance to part with money, drives the needling whine of suspicion that Brooklyn has ignored determinedly all summer to a higher pitch. Trusting by nature, she has never encountered a person she suspects of not being who they say they are. In conventional terms, she knows so little about him, but if he is simply a private person, accusations of dishonesty could put an end to the relationship. Still stupid with love and disarmed by lust, she is not ready to force a full-blown confrontation.

To his annoyance, she starts asking more direct questions but makes little ground. One afternoon, she insists on meeting him spontaneously at his shared flat on the city fringe, to which she has never been invited because they can be uninterrupted at hers. As she laughs off his bad mood, and grandly bows in thanks for satisfying her curiosity, she takes in the industrial chic of a large high-stud, window-lined living space, and the stairs to a mezzanine.

She can see only women's clothes. She can see only one bed. There is a garbled explanation: they are rarely here at the same time, they were in a relationship in the past, they are just friends, it's complicated. He is furious. The next day, she makes the phone call to the only place that can confirm a darker suspicion. The busy receptionist at the creative company is peevish: there isn't anyone who works there by that name.

On the day she prepares to confront him, and expects to break it off, she introduces him for the first time to her parents over dinner. Belatedly, Brooklyn is curious about what they make of him. Her mother has been forewarned of an impending break-up, but wants to meet the person she has heard so much about, even if this is the first and last time. The dinner is bizarre, but accomplished without drama. Her parents are friendly and polite, he is charming but clearly rattled, and Brooklyn is completely preoccupied by how to challenge him after they leave.

Conversation on the walk back to Brooklyn's apartment is awkward, stilted — they are both out of sorts. By the time they are standing face to face in her bedroom, when she has steeled her nerves for a long and ugly showdown, it suddenly becomes apparent that he will not allow her even this. Her first questions meet an impenetrable wall. He will not meet her eyes. There are no explanations or defence — he will not fight, for any of it. He agrees it's over between them.

―――

Brooklyn has already given up the lease on her apartment and must now find another. She can neither afford nor stomach the apartment they were to share, and forfeits her deposit. She walks the steep hill to explore the top of main street, its grubby cafes, vintage shops, and Asian supermarket, and adapts to the hip, alternative vibe. When she strides across the pebble-grey marble foyer of a former department store, and dashes up the grand staircase into a loft apartment ahead of a horde of would-be renters behind her, she announces to the agent that she will take it before she has even seen the mezzanine bedroom.

Once settled, she delights in the rolling green expanses of the city domain close by, and the beauty of her home in the old landmark: the aqua-trimmed Art Deco columns lining the ground floor entrance, the warmth of opal globes greeting her at the foot of the English oak staircase, the enveloping flood of light from the wall of windowpanes when she walks through her front door.

When novelty has worn, she is struck by piercing loneliness, and distracts herself with glamour. No longer a poorly paid bookdealer, she is now a national representative for a major publisher, and flush. Returning from frequent business travel, she spends weekends shopping for a new version of herself in the more upmarket pockets of town: black and white corporate wear, Chanel perfume, old-Hollywood lipstick and red stilettos to match, a crocodile green leather handbag, a yellow chiffon dress like marbled paper that she returns the next day after she notices the exorbitant price tag. She toys with the possibility of re-igniting an old affair, and decides to make space for something real instead.

A few weeks later, strolling hand in hand with the man who will soon be her husband, Brooklyn catches the familiarity of his tall frame out of the corner of her eye, walking in their direction. Always polite, they can't help but say hello, and the moment quickly passes. Later that afternoon, he phones her with something serious to discuss. Protecting her new-found happiness, she refuses to meet him — he must tell her now or not at all.

Something has been bothering him since dinner with her parents: why did she introduce him by that name? The question is so strange and unexpected, she bursts out laughing. Because, she replies, that *is* his name? But it isn't. Stunned, she can only laugh harder at the absurdity. How is it possible that she has known him by the wrong name for over three years? The puzzle is impossible to process on the phone, and she hangs up in astonishment.

Sitting on the edge of the bed, as her jealous new lover

fumes downstairs at the overheard threat of another, she takes herself back to the beginning. The name in the bookshop log, which she asked for once and wrote over and over again. Could she have misheard? The nickname, and others she bestowed on him later, were the only names she ever said aloud. No introductions to friends or family on either side, until the Last Supper. No one by that name at his so-called place of work. Is it possible that their relationship had foundered on such a ridiculous source of confusion? It didn't explain the living arrangements at his flat, or the hidden application form and ID. It didn't explain his vagueness, or unwillingness to share his life outside her apartment. It was all so peculiar and embarrassing, she kept the conundrum to herself.

———

On a whim ten years later, after marriage, divorce, seven relocations, four jobs, and complete surrender to the seductive powers of the internet, Brooklyn indulges her curiosity. She types the unusual first name he gave her on the phone — a name she has never said aloud — and the unusual but uncontentious surname.

He is national news. Credit card fraud involving family members, a wife. She reads the name of a notorious Thai jail. There are mug shots, drug shots, a five-year timeline, and multiple variations of his name. He is walking down a barred corridor, hands cuffed behind his back, face bloodless and surly. He is seated between two local officials, eyes cast down. He will serve years in horrific conditions.

Brooklyn is shocked, saddened, and vindicated. Her Agatha Christie sleuthing was not so ridiculous after all. She is relieved that she was spared worse, unlike so many others close to him, but then she was so talented at draining her own finances that he hardly stood a chance.

BASE CAMP

BLESSING

We married in spite of everything. Our indifference to marriage. Our loathing of wedding ceremonies. The short weeks we had known each other. My family's disapproval. His unspoken unreadiness.

Our new love felt boundless, but our nationalities drew lines around and between us, and so we defied the limits with our own pen and paper, enabling him to stay or me to follow. It felt like us against the world. We were giving our love a chance. Wasn't that the most important thing?

Except marriage, technically speaking, is indifferent to love. In my language, place, and time, marriage is defined in two parts, split cleanly down the middle like a chef's knife through a just-ripe avocado, hitting the hard truth of centre: legal recognition on one side, social sanction on the other.

I had been asked the marriage question twice before. Each time I had answered yes, I will, but not, in the end, I do. Memories of the first proposal vanished without a trace. Memories of the second were lucid and disappointing. This time, in a typical flourish of cocky efficiency, my first attempt at online dating had found love at first sight. His proposal — all heart-pounding cliché and awkwardness on bended knee in public — would be my third and final.

On hearing the news of our engagement, his family appeared simply delighted, and wrapped me warmly into the fold. Mine instantly became a battleground for respect: parental protectiveness, judgement and expectations firing fearful rounds against our speed, rationale, and implications of culture.

It was all too familiar. I had been here before, and chosen to placate family over my desire to marry. This time was different. I was independent and almost 30. I would not be controlled or diminished. I backhanded their objections, and defended the integrity of my beloved and my decision with volcanic fury. I sprinted to enact the most effective solution to the threat of geographical separation that was in my power to provide. In my anger and impatience, I decided my family's blessing was optional.

We married in spite of everything, and for a long time I kept it from them. My family were not there to see us dressed up and love-flushed, speaking vows with eyes locked, exchanging rings of commitment. They were not there to laugh when my gold stiletto stepped on the groom's black polished foot, in the tradition of a Turkish wedding on the other side of the world. We feasted without them at a long, laden table, and then for months we pretended, as if none of it had ever happened.

The deception was sickening, but their ignorance was our cocoon. I sacrificed honesty for control. Our marriage would never have another beginning, and I told myself we couldn't build foundations in an emotional war zone. I naively held out hope that buying time for my family to get to know him might help to smooth the way, but the truth, when it eventually came to light through an unplanned reveal, was devastating.

We sheltered from the fallout by imposing distance: first, a harbour, then a strait, until, for different reasons, we separated ourselves with seas and oceans. Our marriage couldn't be undermined from so far away, but it wasn't relatable either. The home we shared was unfamiliar to them, the pleasant routine of our daily lives unknown. The notion of me as a married woman, when only encountered as an individual, was abstract. Our seclusion protected us, but it also left us vulnerable; in times of marital unsteadiness, my social supports and sense of accountability were limited.

The blessing of my family was optional, but its omission would forever make itself felt, like a piece of shrapnel from a violent act. Marriage for me was a lopsided experience, even after its sad dissolution years later. To me, it would always seem miraculous that I had married the right person, someone I will always respect and cherish. For those closest to me, our marriage will always be a poor decision, a commitment unwitnessed and therefore somehow unreal, an upsetting memory, an awkward topic to be avoided. Half an avocado still tastes like avocado, but it will always be less than the whole.

SELFISH

At first, she wanted six. Her best friend was one of four, and that looked like fun — surely six would be even better. What she wanted most was to name them, and then she would set about discovering their talents and curating their creative lives. Evie, Isabel, Ava, Samuel, Toby, and Sebastian. A writer, a painter, a musician, a dancer, an actor, and one to spare for good measure. Yes, six would cover it. She read a lot of Noel Streatfeild in primary school.

Later, when she realised that having children was less like a project and more like a life commitment, she thought perhaps four — enough people to cosy up around a large wooden kitchen table and fill an old rambling villa on the edge of town. Mention of four raised fewer eyebrows than six, but it still sounded like a lot to many. Evie, Isabel, Toby, and Sebastian. A writer, a painter, a musician, a dancer. Yes, four would be perfect.

Around the time that she might have started having these children, she was curating her own creative life. She was challenging her handspan with the score from *The Piano*, abstracting landscapes on canvas in bold immersive colour, and channelling the Beat poets on a clacking Olivetti. Discovering she had left it a little too late to master ballet, she switched to hip hop, and was learning the lines of *A Respectable Wedding* so she could tiptoe kiss Brecht's bridegroom in drama class. She was consuming languages and history in heaped platefuls daily, breathing art and literature like oxygen.

She began to reconsider. How, with four children, would she have time to continue doing all these things? There was so much that she wanted to do, to be, and she had only just begun. And if *she* could be all these things, why have children at all? She adjusted. Between two and four might be nice, but perhaps one would be sufficient? She supposed she ought to wait and decide with The Other Person, although this approach did not come naturally.

The Other Person, when they revealed themselves in her thirtieth year, was a godsend. Her husband was open-minded, flexible; four sounded rather a lot, but perhaps one or two? As they started down the path of prospective parenthood, they began to pay closer attention to those around them, who were already beyond the point of no return. They silently chalked up the sights and sounds as they socialised with new families, comparing notes and summing up on the drive home, with spurts of horror and fits of laughter as they imagined themselves in the same predicament. Walking through their front door, they would pause to bask in the order and calm, the piles of books they had plentiful time to read, the blessed relief of silence.

It didn't take long to dispel her idyllic notions of a home filled with children; within months of focused observation, she was struggling to make a case for the benefits of motherhood. At best, it would begin with appalling and completely avoidable sources of misery: sleep deprivation, mind-bending noise, mess, restriction, the epic sacrifice of precious time and talent for brain-deadening tasks. If she was lucky, there might be a period of relative calm before the years of teenage stupidity, slammed doors, and shouted disrespect across the generational divide. Perhaps her marriage would be salvageable after the inevitable and irredeemable exchange of passion for domesticity, but this was unlikely. Eventually, the children would leave, only to boomerang back with broken hearts and empty pockets until they were old enough to visit out of duty.

The things other women championed to counter all this — a different kind of love, unconditional, incomparable, primal, fierce, all-consuming — she saw only as debilitating. Her mostly happy childhood memories of family life could not compete, even for a heartbeat, with the joy and drive and strive of her own rich, unburdened adult life. The thought of spending years teaching someone banal skills, when she could be learning wide and high and deep herself, bored her to tears.

She supposed that many who chose to be mothers were seeking to fill a gap in their being that she did not have. She could relate to the romantic tug of procreation, the hazy desire to create something beautiful and alike out of your love for each other, but even this, she suspected, didn't add up. Why, if you loved someone *that* much, treasured what you had together *so* much, would you intentionally commit to a lifestyle that was certain to change you both?

Wrestling with all this, but holding on stubbornly to a strange fascination with pregnancy and the fear of missing out on something she couldn't yet understand, she scanned borrowed books about what to expect until finally she was met, care of a life-saving, no-nonsense author, with the starkest of truths: having a baby is like throwing a grenade into your life. If that's what you want, please proceed to Chapter 2. She read it twice, like a welcome slap across the face. She put the book down and stared out the window, out to sea. Is this what she wanted? Hell no.

The next Saturday morning, as the two of them lazed in bed, balancing books, coffee and croissants, gloriously free to go anywhere and nowhere, do anything and nothing much, she proposed a total retreat. Her research complete, all evidence pointed to the advantages of the status quo. Remarkably, the conversation was brief and without drama. Her husband was somewhat relieved; he too, saw little sense in swapping contentment for a minefield.

The Decision, when others caught wind of it, was met with everything from shrugs to surprise to sadness. Her grandmother labelled her a bluestocking, a badge she accepted with pride. The most irritating response — there's still time to change your mind — she continued to deflect for years. The most outrageous was the rebrand. By choosing to swim against the tide of social expectation, they were no longer a Nice Young Couple — prospective providers of grandchildren, cousins, playmates, consumers, and tax-paying citizens — but Selfish. It wasn't always expressly airborne, but she would forever catch it in the slight frowns of mothers, the sentences left hanging, the polite but vague murmurs that acknowledged but disapproved of her contribution. Its sting was harmless, but it bothered her that it didn't add up.

It appeared that the generally approved guidelines to 'follow your dreams' and 'fulfil your potential' were relevant only until the stage of life when you were best placed to enjoy it and achieve anything of note. At that point, you as an individual became less important than your generic capability to produce another person. The prehistoric rationale, to ensure existence of the species, no longer rang true; any child she produced would be environmentally surplus to requirements. Instilling superiority in self-sacrifice for a person you yourself created was a nonsense she associated with tired Christian values. Contributing to the government's economies of scale at the expense of liveable cities made little sense either. She was not obliged to entertain any parent who would be otherwise crushed at the prospect of life without grandchildren — they could find something else to do.

She would, mercifully, not be joining The Club, recent members of which were doubling down on self-sabotage by choosing a child-parent partnership model. It was a rare thing to finish a cup of coffee before it was cold, or hold an uninterrupted conversation with an adult. Constructive discipline was a dying art. Children once instructed to be 'seen and not heard' were now the fickle sun around which adults revolved, encouraged to 'speak their words' regardless of who else was already speaking. Their parents — otherwise competent employees, business owners, highly-trained specialists — were now so hobbled by being responsive at knee height that they struggled to achieve low-level goals like getting out the door on time.

She would not grieve the loss of membership, but her friendships with mothers would long suffer a disconnect; she could not relate to their tales of bringing up, bedding down, and fielding crises in miniature. In turn, their eyes would glaze over at the question of what they were reading, what films they had seen lately, what their career plans were for the year ahead, as if she were speaking in a language they once knew but had forgotten.

She would resent the constant disruptions in the workplace, when parenting colleagues arrived late and exhausted, or dropped everything early to run little people between school and sports. When annoyance got the better of her, she would question them about the benefits of parenthood, if they ever wished they had chosen the other path. Almost without exception, they swerved the questions defensively as if avoiding a pile up on the motorway and toed the line: they couldn't imagine life without their children now. It was against Club Rules to answer any other way.

After decades of being without, she would still be unable to summon a single example of how her life would be better with children. It would amaze her that despite so many questionable life decisions, she had got this one so absolutely right. By then, she and her husband had sadly but amicably gone their separate ways, uncoupling without complication to pursue lives in different hemispheres and achieve ambitions unfettered. By then, she had learned the word for her emotional overwhelm, and suspected that motherhood would have made it even harder to balance on a tightrope between the poles of depression and hypomania, the falls more damaging.

She lived in an old house on the edge of town, where she hosted dinner parties for her friends at a large wooden kitchen table. She started weekdays at her writing desk, contentedly following her dream and fulfilling her potential. On rainy weekend mornings she played piano, before hanging her coat on the back of the door of the garden shed to paint at her easel in joyful bursts. She had cultivated a passion for gardening — a new way of painting on a grand scale — and spent fair weather days in a state of timeless, blissful industry.

When she wasn't captivated in the dress circle of a theatre at night, she feasted on history and literature from the bookshelves in every room as if her life depended on it, which it did. At the age of 46 she had bought the house from an elderly woman she didn't know, who insisted there was still time to change her mind; surely she didn't want to spend the rest of her life here alone without children? Actually, yes, she replied, that sounds nice and quiet. That would suit her just fine.

TRANSPORTED

There is a risk attached to immersing yourself in the history of a new place before you visit. If, like me, you are inclined to romanticise the past, it can be difficult to align your sepia imaginings with the garish realities of the present. First sighting a country through the eyes of a passionate historian and patriot far from home is bound to skew expectations, but I have only myself to blame. As someone who has been travelling the world since childhood, my naivete never ceases to astonish me.

I come to know Turkey first through love, and through him the landscapes of its poetry and music, its decorative arts and imperial past. I first trace its contours from the other side of the world, dipping fingertips into cool, white ceramic, seduced by the gloss of tulips and carnations in red, blue and green. Through southern hemisphere windows, sunlight spins off necklaces of gifted gold and traditional wedding silver, palm-sized patterned mirrors turned to the wall. The sounds that fill our home are the soulful twang and pluck of strings across wide wooden bellies — the bağlama, the ud — the calming waver of the shepherd's flute, the occasional proclamation of the high-pitched zurna.

My love paints my mind's eye with rich tapestries, intricate histories of diverse communities across the Ottoman Empire, from seventeenth-century Hungary, east to Armenia, south to Egypt. Between his tales, I feast on a lavish magazine for connoisseurs of Turkey, until the pull to see for myself becomes so insistent that I commence a campaign of persuasion to move. On a weekend drive inland, into the mountainous Otago territory I worship for its contrast to the lush coastal green I take for granted — temples of schist and tussock, grand sweeps of dry plain — he says, it is like this where we are going.

With travel imminent, language comes into sharp relief. I reshape my lips, train my tongue to navigate the twists of a new alphabet. I linger at our doors, windows, cupboards and furniture to sound the phonetic words written on affixed paper squares. I practise stringing phrases like beads at mealtimes, slowly, like a clumsy child, stretching the patience of my beloved, who holds claim to a richer store of English vocabulary than I. His parents, also far from home, are more easily impressed, still wrestling as they are with English themselves. My progress is too slow to build impressive cultural bridges, but our closeness is strengthened as I find my balance on river stones, one word at a time.

Perched on a hill in my capital city, in the kitchen of a Turkish ambassador's far-flung outpost, I study the smooth, confident hands of my mother-in-law as she rolls warm pilaf in vine leaves and feta in filo, softens the rough strangeness of okra with steaming, seasoned tomatoes. As she works, I learn the contents of a Central Anatolian pantry in her native tongue: peppers, chillis, sumac, mint, parsley, walnut, pistachio, pomegranate. I do not share her patience for peeling, layering, and simmering, and eat better than I cook, but her lessons will serve me well in the markets that await me. She must sigh inwardly at our bland, lacklustre ingredients, but I am spoiled with the fruits of her mastery, and the love and goodwill that infuses them.

On arrival in Istanbul, en route to Ankara, primed for bookmarked beauty and grandeur, my first impression is shock. The hand-tinted landscape of my historied imagination, lantern-lit and bejewelled with architectural feats, is instantly blighted by the gaudy colours of concrete apartment blocks, scattershot across the arid stretch between the airport and the city. These, I will soon discover, are a common sight, and the scale of unlovely modernity is dispiriting.

The aesthetic jolt is reminiscent of my arrival in China, after a year of similarly selective immersion in a bygone era, and I feel foolish to have made the same mistake twice. In all the months I have been armchair travelling Turkey with the eye of a curator, I have given little thought to contemporary lifestyle. I know vaguely where we are to live, but I am unprepared for the visual impact of apartments like ours en masse.

Had I approached the country as a short-term tourist, the city surrounds might have barely registered, but I was a resident, and this was to be my home. Had I not been running from distress, the bloody abandonment of a dream job in publishing still dripping from my fingers, I would not have heaped my hopes for emotional deliverance at the feet of a foreign country. As I swallow the first dose of reality, and adjust my rose-coloured glasses, there is nothing to say aloud that will not offend. I sink silently into the backseat of the car and the swirl of rapid chatter between brothers long separated.

The next morning, on the Asian side of the Bosphorus, I wake with alarm to a loudspeaker, its strangled announcement so harsh that I am slow to recognise the call to prayer. I had imagined a gentle awakening by an ancient muezzin, calling wholeheartedly without assistance from the balcony of a minaret, but I do not resent the early start on a mild winter's day. I am eager to explore the riches of the city, in the hope of restoring my inspiration, and warding off the depression that is threatening to take hold. Across the strait, a heady banquet of pattern, stone, tile and arabesque awaits — palaces, churches, mosques, the glowing vaulted maze of the Grand Bazaar — but first, a ferry guided by seagulls, chilled hands warmed by pretzels and strong tea in tulip glass.

To my dismay, many of the city's treasures remain just out of reach. Ironically, it is my love, the historian, who inadvertently stands between us. Reunions with friends take precedence, and I am surprised to discover that my husband is uncomfortable with the idea of me sightseeing alone. It is trying to sit and smile politely, playing the dutiful wife between hurried glimpses of the famous city; it is like being fed titbits under the table when I am ravenous.

    I distract myself with the best food I have ever tasted: the dense comfort of street-side su boreği and gözleme, the simple satisfaction of yoghurt lentil soup in bustling diners, the salted crunch of fresh fish baguettes at tiny tables on the quay. I tell myself that I live here now, that we can visit again another time. I can't explain my sense of urgency to know the city without betraying my first impression. I can't explain that I need to connect to history and beauty like others need friends and community. I can't share my premonition that I will need reasons to stay in Turkey, that our future here together depends on it.

I am soothed by the drive to Ankara through a quiet winter palette of sky, forest, and snow. My heart lifts with the restorative natural balance of low-lying towns and villages in weathered stone and brick, dwarfed by vast plateau. I want to drive for days, weeks, but we are tethered to commitments in the capital.

We soon find ourselves at home, on an elevated street named after a famous Ottoman poet, in a sleepy suburb that looks east to the mountains. It is a view I will drink in many times throughout the day, deaf to requests to close the sheer curtains for privacy, as is customary.

We are grateful for use of the family apartment, and the freedom to redecorate. We liberate space and inject colour, drawing for inspiration on the chocolate wood and whitewashed walls of Ottoman Turkish townhouses. We create a haven suited to the quiet industry of a freelance editor and ambitious scholar. The dry, predictable climate makes for weeks of uninterrupted sunshine, filling our rooms and buoying my spirits.

Compared to densely populated Istanbul, Ankara is relatively calm, and an easy city to navigate and learn. For several weeks, I weave my way down the hills to the centre, aboard easy-going minivans and the sedate local bus. I explore the shopping district surrounding the university where I study Turkish, observing and adapting to pace and customs in an effort to blend in. I am dark-haired and almost look the part, but give myself away by smiling at strangers; I am told that I should be more guarded, or I might invite trouble.

By spring, I have established a daily routine, jogging a morning route between sparse green spaces, working from home, and stocking up at the local grocers. I stay in touch with a friend from university, but mostly keep to myself. Coming from a small family who rarely visits relatives, I am unprepared for the expectations of an extended Turkish family, who cheerfully visit in groups at short notice. I suppose they think I must be lonely, but the invasion of occupied solitude, and burden of hospitality in a foreign language is a strain. After my first failed attempt to make the required quality or quantity of Turkish tea, I cede the kitchen to more qualified aunts, and accept the role of serving girl.

On weekends, I naturally gravitate north to the dusty heart of old Ankara, overlooked by a seventh-century citadel. Here, I am transported by museums, shops jumbled with antiques and traditional crafts, and performances at the State Opera and Ballet. My insistence on travelling there alone, rather than waiting for my protective, time-poor husband strains the atmosphere, but it is in Ulus that I feel the pulse of the country I have longed to meet. In my mind, I reverently touch the ground each time I step off the bus. After a few hours of being lost in time, I return home inspired and recount the highlights, easing the tension between us.

We are both so enchanted by the past that it contributes to our downfall. My beloved, joyfully buried in books and bound to the demands of academic research, cannot be torn away, and so our journeys beyond the city boundaries to places I long to see are few and far between. As our second winter comes to a close, I admit to the crushing depression that has been feeding off the soulless suburb in which we live, and the whittling away of our marriage with the tools of neglect.

The Turkish government has clamped down on freedom of speech, and the think tank that has kept me in work has gone underground. Drained by disappointment, my motivation to learn the language has faded, limiting my ability to pursue a more independent life within reach, while we take time to consider our options. We begin to wrestle with the prospect of my permanent departure.

Years later, I still think of him often, his eyes alight, tracing Ottoman script in gilt or stone with his fingertips as we pass a historic site. He is sitting in our Turkish kitchen, bursting with the seventeenth century, regaling me with tales of Edirne over breakfast; I am piling my plate with salty black olives, hard-boiled egg, feta, sweet cucumber, scented tomato, dripping honeycomb, and fresh bread from the simit seller that we hauled up in a basket that morning.

I see him standing, head cocked, captivated by the murmurs of an elderly shopkeeper in the old town of Urgup; I am surrounded by rough barrels of heavenly fruit dried on rooftops, reliving a day of fairy chimneys, rock-cut Byzantine chapels and glass mosaic lanterns. I think of my beloved, writing Ottoman history on the other side of the world, as I furnish my southern home of dark wood and painted white walls, conjuring the Turkey of my imagination with floral fabrics, carpets, and ceramics in red, blue and green.

HAUNTED

You always take your bag when you leave a building, even if you're just stepping out. You choose the stairs over lifts. You keep your phone well charged, and your petrol tank full. When you walk through a city, you're aware of concrete overhangs, the possibility of falling masonry. You understand what liquefaction means, and you didn't learn it from a book. You can estimate magnitude. You know when to keep calm and carry on.

Standing in front of a stark new build each time you return to Christchurch, this is not what you see. You see the sweat-crafted beauty of weathered stone, cast iron, and stained glass that soaked up stories of place for over a century. You see what was there before.

You recall a two-storey brick cottage by the Avon, a pleasant riverside walk from town, like something out of a Jane Austen novel. Garden pockets of winter roses, the scent of the old lilac bush that perfumed the front rooms, and the surprise of strawberries by the gate.

You remember the gentle companionship of the tree that

dappled the arch of light across your desk in Cashel Mall, and the ring-ring rumble of the inner-city tram beneath your window — all high-gloss paint, waxed wood, and copper polished to a shine. You hear the hum of a life that was cordoned off and red-zoned, demolished and removed, never to be lived again. You summon historic events that collapsed history.

Newcomers to the city, looking for a place to take root, see a silent square gap between houses, overgrown with weeds. You see a late summer garden liquefied, soil-squeezed water gushing down the driveway and onto the street.

You watch the protective sway and shudder of a grand old weatherboard villa from the relative shelter of a kauri doorway. Bookshelves crashing, a bedroom wall cleaved down the middle, the squeal of the wooden stairwell in your ears. The landing is warped, the veranda is hobbled, you wonder if your bed could fall through the floor.

Downstairs, the kitchen is possessed. Cupboards are hurling glass, tins, and packets of rice across the room and all over the floor. In the lounge, rejected picture frames are smashed and splintered, the pink glass chandelier is looped and confused.

Outside, the river bridge is twisting like a corkscrew. Cars are bouncing in car parks, alarms are blaring, sirens are wailing emergency. Buildings are rubbled, roads creviced, buses crushed, hills are sliding into suburbs. Power out, phones running low, no drinking water from the taps. People are disconnected, animals disoriented. Hearts are breaking. Hearts stop.

September. February. June. For months, the city is brought to its knees, pounded to dust by quakes and aftershocks. The place you have chosen to rebuild your life from ground zero will take decades to rebuild itself. Your grief is silent but inconsolable. Landmarks are lost, bungalow-lined streets flattened, infrastructure crippled, the city plan in disarray. Christchurch resembles a war zone.

Its soul retreats to the remnants: what's left of the old university and the Botanic's centenarian trees. It lies low in the pool of the Peacock Fountain, and hides beneath the punts in the Boatsheds. On the worst days, it decamps to the outskirts: mourning on the edges of rivers and lakes, wallowing ankle-deep in coastal tides, weeping on the jetties of Diamond Harbour. You will sit in these places, heart-wrenched and fearful, each time you break your promise to never return.

―――

Had you prompted me with the word *haunted* before the Christchurch earthquakes, I would have told you a story of a different time and place, a different river Avon, on the other side of the world.

Where others looked into a pane of glass, and saw the other side of a room reflected, I once saw a stunted old woman, the colour and texture of storm clouds, staring back. Rumour had it that her name was Alice, and I had waited a long time to meet her. She took me by surprise at the witching hour, as I cleaned the bathroom mirrors in the sixteenth-century attic. I had expected to see her in the heavy-beamed front room on the first floor overlooking Sheep Street — the room where I always felt cold.

Perhaps it was only in the early hours of the morning that we were ever going to meet. The Stratford restaurant was usually bustling with preparation or theatre-going patrons, the promise of the play to come, and the rowdy deconstructions that followed. Where does an old ghost go then? Can Alice visit other Tudor houses that line the street to the river? Does she linger in the gods of the Royal Shakespeare or rest under the stage at the Swan? Or are we forever bound to haunt the place where a part of us has died?

FLOURISH

WEEK 0

I am woken before sunrise by the voices of angels floating amidst the spires. Perhaps I am dreaming, but I release the iron latch of my tower room window to let them in, all the same. I am slow to recall that my first Sunday in Oxford is May Day, the first day of spring. Later, I will discover that it is the Magdalen College choir, singing from the top of the Great Tower as it has done since the sixteenth century, but for now I simply lie still in my narrow scholar's bed, eyes closed, enchanted.

At seven o'clock, I am gently returned to the physical realm: the pealing of church bells takes over from the voices, birds take over from the bells, street bands from the birds. The day is all celebration and sunshine, but I have work to do; Tuesday is the start of Trinity Term, and the deadline for my first assignment.

I turn over in bed to consider the books stacked with care on my desk. Six bound in leather and vellum are seventeenth-century treasures on loan from my tutor across the Quad. Others are modern publications from the College library — the first of many on twelve daunting but thrilling reading lists. I have a few hours until brunch in Hall, and plenty of time to make progress. I take a few steps north to the shower, a few steps south to the kettle, a few steps east to the desk, and I am ready to begin.

I am living in an ivory tower, near the top of a winding stone stairwell, above the Porter's Lodge of fourteenth-century New College. I am starting my day on the other side of the world from the earthquaked city I decamped from just over a week ago. My presence here is completely unexpected, and nothing short of miraculous.

Having taken the leap from full-time employment to full-time postgraduate studies, my first year at University of Canterbury in New Zealand had been derailed on the second day of term. The first day had been full of promise: a new Digital Humanities lab, gleaming slick with brushed-silver hardware, was to be the playground for early adopters of a new academic programme. A list of intriguing assignments opened up a whole new world for the exploration of digitised cultural heritage collections. There were flickers of friendship in a motley crew of curious and creative Honours students. Day two: a massive earthquake close to the centre of Christchurch — chaos, carnage, a city in crisis. Large white tents popped up in campus car parks, keeping students and staff at a safe distance from hazardous concrete stairwells, dominoed bookshelves, and shattered windows.

As we braced ourselves between every aftershock for a make-do year studying from our damaged homes, an incredible rumour began to circulate: the University of Oxford had reached out to Canterbury with thirty funded places for Honours students in the Humanities. The news, when confirmed, so challenged my quake-rattled comprehension that I couldn't process it for several hours. I was so stunned by the enormity and strangeness of the opportunity, that instead of submitting the application immediately, I cleaned the house.

When I eventually sat down to apply, the form was straightforward: some basic details, a brief description of my academic and professional ambitions, and space to list my choice of courses. For an English Literature graduate and former rare bookdealer, the course catalogue was a smorgasbord from heaven, and I piled my plate high with palaeography, bibliography, English standardisation, and history of the *Oxford English Dictionary*. I waxed lyrical about my passion for cultural heritage, and my intention to contribute to the digitisation of collections in New Zealand. I cried from start to finish.

The weeks following acceptance were a blur, clouded by an urgent operation that sliced me hip to hip. I was released from hospital stitched, swollen, and barely able to carry a suitcase, but by Easter Monday I was here in my tower room, with the gift of ten fully funded weeks to live my wildest dream. I had been allocated to New College along with two other Canterbury students. Over the course of the term, we would come to know other colleges as the headquarters of our peers placed elsewhere.

Oxford is not new to me, but until now I have known it only from the outside, stealing glimpses of life inside college walls from cobbled streets and quiet lanes. Familiarity has been helpful, enabling me to sidestep jetlagged overwhelm and hit the academic ground running. I have fallen back into the hybrid accent of my childhood years in London and early twenties in Stratford-upon-Avon, adapting my vowels so that I may be better understood. At 35, my age suggests tutor rather than a student, but otherwise I almost blend in.

My window is opened wide over Holywell Quad, framing the medieval city wall that runs through the College, and the spring-bright fields in the north-east beyond. I am fortunate to have been assigned a room of my own: a spartan, quiet space in the heart of the city. I have only to read, write, listen, debate, and learn; everything but my laundry is taken care of by the friendly Scouts in housekeeping and cooks in Hall. Such an arrangement feels both novel and necessary, given the intensive schedule of assignments, tutorials, lectures, and seminars ahead; I will be working harder than I ever have before to keep up.

By the end of the eight-week term, I will have researched, written and discussed nine essays on topics almost entirely new to me, and completed code-breaked transcriptions of historical manuscripts in Elizabethan handwriting, but on the first Sunday in May, this is hard to imagine. Right now, I need to find a magnifying glass, a Latin dictionary, a pencil sharpener, and breakfast.

WEEK 1

It is Thursday afternoon, and I am drinking tea with the New College Warden and his wife in one of the oldest, permanently occupied houses in England. I am here at their generous invitation for a tour of the Lodgings and private garden — a delightful diversion in a busy day of fast-paced lectures and frantic reading. It is just the moment when cucumber sandwiches might be expected, and I am not disappointed.

I am seated, shoulders back, ankles crossed, on the edge of a chintz sofa with porcelain teacup and saucer in hand, answering polite but painful questions about the devastation in Christchurch. It is the last thing I want to speak of in this bubble of perfection, but it is the reason that I am here after all, and so the bubble must burst for the duration of a teapot. I discretely find solace in the room's sublime architectural details, glimpses of seventeenth-century "modernisations" in the space between the seated Warden and his wife, taking care not to appear distracted.

Soon, I will be rewarded with access to the secret garden behind the barn and stables on New College Lane. As my eyes stray to the window, a favourite childhood story, *The Warden's Niece*, floats to the surface, and my heart cartwheels at the realisation that I am living the fantasy of my ten-year-old self. I cannot imagine an Oxford experience more quintessential than this, until I find myself, on the second Sunday in May, a black-gowned guest of honour at High Table in Hall.

It is claimed that New College, inspired by the fourteenth-century palace at Windsor, is the most widely copied university college in England. Its striking architecture, stone masonry, and stained-glass windows are daily food for the soul, and the routine of communal meals in the medieval Dining Hall is a feast for the senses. Each day, I sit down with up to two hundred of my fellow students at long wooden tables, occasionally making conversation, but mostly taking in the details: linenfold panelling and giant oak beams, lofty stone-arched windows and painted crests, gilt-framed portraits of past wardens.

For the past week, I have indulged in three hot meals a day and, more often than not, dessert with lunch and dinner. The menus vary with everything from curries and chilli to pasta and risotto, but there is a much-appreciated emphasis on traditional English standards that evoke my grandmothers' kitchens: roast beef, new potatoes, beans, cabbage, and steaming boats of gravy, trifle, steamed pudding, fruit crumble, and heavy jugs of cream and custard.

Dinner is served both early and late, and Informal Hall best suits my early-to-rise routine, but tonight is Formal Hall and I'm sitting with the grown-ups. High Table runs along a dais at the head of the hall, overlooking a sea of low-lit lamps, polished glassware, and black-gowned students. The scene is somewhat intimidating, and I'm thankful to be seated with my back to the crowd, opposite a friendly Mathematics Fellow, who turns out to be a splendid conversationalist. The food is magnificent, the wine flows freely, and since I'm clearly having such a wonderful time, it doesn't end there.

With three courses complete, the High Table guests are silently and almost imperceptibly ushered into line, to retrace the formal procession that commenced the evening. My scintillating dinner companion offers me an impromptu tour of the Senior Common Room, smoking room and reading room — an inner sanctum for the College Fellowship that most students never set eyes on until they butterfly into alumni.

The beauty of the candlelit Common Room, edged with panelling, paintings, and jewel-coloured carpets, is breathtaking. Windows are opened to the College garden and the perfume of wisteria that hangs lilac and lovely from the historic walls. Soft voices from deep, wingback armchairs weave between antique oak furniture and leatherbound books, like the steady burble of a stream. A long side table is laid with coffee and petit fours, and I am encouraged to partake. I have died and gone to heaven on what my grandmother would call a red-letter day.

WEEK 2

It is Tuesday morning in the basement of the New College library, where I am sliding heavy bookshelves back and forth along the rails. I am sleuthing around seventeenth-century booksellers and printers, in an effort to complete my second book history essay by this afternoon. Occasional words are exchanged with a helpful librarian, but I am otherwise alone, dipping in and out of Term Catalogues and the Stationers Company Register, as I type frantic paragraphs in footnote-heavy pages.

I enjoy working from the College library, which is cosier upstairs. It is small enough to be homely, and large enough to be useful, but it is not my only port of call. The University boasts over one hundred libraries, more than twenty of which are part of the famous Bodleian, and I work from several. Time-pressured essay production relies on immediate access to reading list material, some of which can only be read on site, and I often start the day outside a library, waiting for the doors to open.

The English Faculty library, which is larger and more modern but less inspiring, is my engine room. I make the short walk from college several times a week for a fresh stack of books, and lectures in the adjoining theatres, taking a left turn near the Morris Garages, and slowing down to admire the medieval tower of St Cross Church. If time allows, I divert briefly from the crossroads to St Catherine's and visit a friend studying Art History, surrounded by Danish modernist architecture and museum-worthy sculpture.

When my reading list points me in the direction of the History Faculty collections, I work from the majestic eighteenth-century Radcliffe Camera, which links to the Old Bodleian underground. It's hard to believe that I don't work from my favourite windowed niche of the Upper Rad Cam every day, but the iconic circular library, with its Neo-Classical arches and decorative dome, is so spectacular that I find it difficult to concentrate on reading.

One day, the books come to me, transported on a clattering library trolley by a tutor who dismisses the advantages of digitised texts. Arriving at his lounge-like study in Long Barn, I am greeted by a great pile of eighteenth-century leatherbound dictionaries and English grammars sitting in the middle of the carpet, haloed by the afternoon sun. I am like a child on Christmas morning, unsure which to open first. A knee-balanced folio or a hand-held octavo? Samuel Johnson or Nathan Bailey?

Tomorrow is tutorial day, with History of the Book in the morning and English Standardization in the afternoon. Some Oxford students attend tutorials with one or two of their peers, but I am tutored one-on-one. The tutorial approach, which takes the form of a free-flowing discussion, is promoted as a relaxed forum in which to explore ideas and develop confidence. I find it difficult to defend what I feel are my broad, rushed, and scantily-researched essays, but I enjoy learning by listening, as my tutors respond and paint a more colourful and intricate picture of the world in which I am only dipping my toes.

On Thursday, after two weeks of full immersion, intense study, and injustice to the outstanding spring weather, I declare it time for a field trip. I set out on foot from the English Faculty, passing University Parks, on a pilgrimage to what was once the home of James Murray's Scriptorium on the Banbury Road, and the birthplace of the *Oxford English Dictionary*. I'm not sure what I expected, but I suppose I was hoping for a taste of time-travel, so the reality of standing outside someone else's unloved home over a century later is an anti-climax. I backtrack to St Giles' and the legendary Eagle and Child pub, to sit with my disappointment, a half-pint lager shandy, and the ghosts of Tolkien and C.S. Lewis.

Refreshed and regrouped, I head out and around the corner into Jericho to pay homage to Oxford University Press. After this afternoon's exploration I will return to these streets often, sauntering along Little Clarendon and Walton Street, criss-crossing between the Albion Beatnik Bookstore, the Phoenix Picturehouse, Italian and French bistros, and succulent Greek feasts at Cafe Manos. Today, I soak up the sunshine, scope out the territory, and make plans for a tour of the Press Museum with friends in tow. The quiet, bohemian suburb of Jericho is a town-and-gown hybrid, which has the pleasant effect of loosening one's tie a little, and I instantly feel at home.

On my way back, just a few minutes shy of New College, I make a final stop at Blackwell's bookshop on Broad Street. The first two floors are bustling and brimming with shiny new covers. I head upstairs to the relative hush of the rare book room, where I want to buy almost everything and buy nothing, leaving with the contentment that comes from being surrounded by words on paper. I arrive back in time for dinner in Hall, and an evening's reconnaissance into seventeenth-century authorship, censorship, copyright and clandestine publishing.

WEEK 3

An assorted group of bibliographers, librarians, and literary devotees has gathered for a talk on Jane Austen's *Volume the First* — a compilation of her early short works and a recent conservation project. Those of us on time are seated on dark wooden pews, either side of the narrow seventeenth-century room that is Convocation House. Latecomers are entering through a door off the Divinity School, Oxford's oldest teaching room.

At the north end, natural light plays in the pocket squares of glass that make up generous stone-arched windows. Above our heads, on the other side of the Gothic fan-vaulted ceiling, is the Duke Humphrey's Library, the oldest reading room in the Bodleian. We are awaiting the arrival of Professor Kathryn Sutherland, who will take command of the historic room from the flagstones, below the Vice-Chancellor's throne.

Today's talk is one of several opportunities I have taken to venture beyond the standard fare of lectures and tutorials, and the rooms of New College and the English Faculty. Open invitations to enthusiasts like me are plentiful, and I keep a watchful eye on noticeboards and mailing lists for events of interest. I am finding this the best way to meet academics and professional staff, who are closer to my age, and often connected with Digital Humanities initiatives across the University. Such events open doors to other colleges, and spaces behind the ropes of a public tour.

Earlier in the term, taking a break from an essay on printer William Caxton, I stretched my legs down Longwall Street, up the High, and around the corner to Christ Church. Skirting the Saturday morning tourists milling around outside Tom Gate, I presented myself to a bowler-hatted Porter, who pointed me in the direction of a lecture room across the quad.

I had arrived early for a colloquium on the fourteenth-century production and circulation of the Wycliffe Bible, allowing me time to explore, so I took the long way around the central fountain and a graceful heron, which I initially mistook for a statue. I found the sumptuous Cathedral, where I stood in the nave appropriately transfixed, before heading towards the Dining Hall, and oil paintings in the McKenna Room. As I ventured upstairs, my pretended nonchalance gave way at the jaw-dropping beauty of the ceiling above, and when I stopped in my tracks I was promptly questioned by an eagle-eyed Porter, thinking I was a tourist out of bounds.

On Thursday I find myself back at Merton, which sits serenely beside Christ Church Meadow, Oxford Botanic Garden, and the meandering River Cherwell. A previous seminar in the TS Eliot Theatre, on the Royal Society Library, had led to a lively discussion and invitation to today's Digital Humanities workshop. I am sitting like a sponge at a long wooden table with heavyweights in my field — the authors of work that I will later cite — drinking in every word and taking notes as calmly as I am affecting to be. This workshop will lead to further College visits thanks to a friendly Fellow, and a gatecrashed Bodleian project launch that will inspire the trajectory of my academic research for the next five years.

WEEK 4

Mid-term, the weather turns blustery and my tower room is suddenly cold. I bookmark a doorstopper Cambridge *History of Libraries* and run downstairs in search of warmer clothes. A good excuse to splurge on some New College merchandise, I make a dash for the Broad Street shops, returning windswept in a crested navy-blue hoodie. After Informal Hall (roast lamb and apple crumble), I am sufficiently warm and fortified to settle down for a night of reading.

Until today, I have walked the College Garden most evenings, greeting the new blooms as they paint the borders: waist-high bearded irises cloaked in velvet purple, the bold pink of seductive peonies, two-tone tulips, and giant poppies splashing orange. I follow the wide gravel path between the old city wall and the expansive manicured lawn, turning in behind the mysterious tree-covered Mound, with its stone steps to nowhere. The garden is always quiet after dinner and I circle it slowly, appreciating the great canopy of leaves that I imagine must be especially glorious in the autumn.

When I need to stretch my legs in the heat of the day, I choose the opposite end of the College, taking a turn in the cool of the Cloisters next to the Chapel. Occasionally, I am treated to a performance by the choir boys practising in a room nearby, each note crisper and clearer here than the muted strains that reach my bedroom window. The all-male choir of New College is world renowned, and I have heard them in full glory in the Chapel, raising Handel's *Messiah* high to the historic beams, but I enjoy these unexpected snatches of music more, the young voices enriching the atmosphere as I go about my day.

By mid-week, I have submitted my essay on the history of public libraries, and commenced transcription of Early

Modern texts. My tutor has primed me with a seventeenth-century crash course in calligraphy, care of English writing master Martin Billingsley and his 1618 copybook *The Pens Excellencie*. There is no time to learn about the cutting of quills, but I am soon familiar with the flow and flourish of ink in Secretary Hand. As I trace the dips and swirls of the alphabet with my index finger, there are echoes of childhood: memories of playing with leftover sheets of Letraset, and watching the freehand skills of my father — a graphic designer and talented calligrapher.

Now, my tutor feeds my inbox with a selection of digitised archival documents to transcribe. The challenges lie in decoding the informalities and individual quirks of each writer, their speed and slant, the instances of copybook divergence. Meaning can hide behind historical context, unfamiliar spelling, and archaic language, or be lost in the fading of ink, or wear of paper.

I begin with the briefest and least intimidating — a recipe for quince preserve — which I promptly dispatch. This is followed by a letter dated 1576, and instructions for Privy Council. I am enjoying myself until I graduate to the last will and testament of bible translator, Member of Parliament, and former Warden of Merton, Sir Henry Savile. The document is epic and rambling beyond belief, but I make a decent fist of it, and my tutor is suitably impressed.

WEEK 5

Trinity Term is in full swing, and the week glitters with agreeable distractions. A much-anticipated tour of Oxford University Press Museum reveals the famous Mouse's Tale type for *Alice in Wonderland*, and original quotation slips sent to the Scriptorium by members of the public for the *Oxford English Dictionary*. I am so happy that I don't want to leave, and slip into the staff cafeteria for a pot of tea, pretending for a stolen moment that I work there.

In search of a book in the Balfour Library, I encounter the dinosaurs and striking Victorian architecture of Pitt Rivers Museum, with its stunning glass and iron roof recalling images of the Crystal Palace. Later, I wine and dine with my fellow Cantabrians at the kindly Vice-Chancellor's home on the Banbury Road, and indulge in some metaphorical tie-loosening at Jericho Tavern.

Thursday takes me to London, which is bulging at the seams with high-season tourists. I make short work of the Charing Cross Road bookshops, National Gallery, and British Museum, before an exhilarating meeting of Digital Humanities scholars at the University of London. I tidy my frenzied notes into a report for academic counterparts in New Zealand, before re-focusing on my Oxford studies.

The weather rights itself in time for the Summer Eights — the annual intercollegiate regatta. From my tower, I can hear the roar of the crowds along the Isis, cheering the rowers battling it out in college colours for Head of the River. Motivated by my rapid progress, I am committed to transcription, but I don't resent the excuse to avoid the Meadow on one of the busiest weeks of the year. I prefer to visit the home of lazy punts and cheerful houseboats, Longhorn cows and storybook squirrels in peace, when time allows for a leisurely walk with Cornish ice-cream in hand.

Come Sunday, I am sprawled beneath my open window, catching my breath between the pages of Evelyn Waugh before immersing myself in another essay. A group of students is mucking about with a game of croquet on the lawn below, which is what I might be doing with friends at Magdalen, but I am perfectly content to enjoy the summer's evening from here. My bedside table, dusty with biography, *Brideshead Revisited*, and

Zuleika Dobson, has been unsuccessfully competing with the stuff of reading lists since I arrived.

WEEK 6

As Trinity Term lectures wind down, my schedule eases, but I feel somewhat bereft. The rapid pace of learning that my lecturers expect and enable is invigorating. Experts in their field, at the top of their game, it is an honour to watch them in full stride. They are joyful and generous, but there is no dumbing down, spelling out, accommodation of the unprepared. As students, we are responsible for our own foundational knowledge, and expected to arrive informed and ready to follow and participate in whip-smart critical thinking. I am in my element, and sorry to let go.

Some of my Canterbury colleagues are exploring ways to stay, others are looking to academic opportunities in Europe and elsewhere in the UK. In a final lecture, I learn of new postgraduate courses on offer, and funded internships at Oxford University Press. I am tempted, but for reasons that will baffle me later, choose not to pursue either. An idea for research is beginning to emerge, which I envisage applying to cultural heritage collections at home.

I take the train to Stratford-upon-Avon, for a day of nostalgia amongst my old haunts. I tour the impressive extensions and improvements to the Royal Shakespeare Theatre, where I am surprised and delighted to be recognised from my days serving pints at The Dirty Duck.

Like London, Stratford is heaving with tourists, reminding me of the relief that settles on the town in winter, when locals don't have to navigate swarms of camera-clicking pedestrians to get from A to B. The bustle is tiresome, the weather bitterly cold, and melancholy gets the better of me. By late afternoon,

I am relieved to return to the tranquillity behind Oxford college walls.

WEEK 7

I wake on Monday to the distressing news of further destruction in Christchurch: another severe earthquake and massive aftershocks wreaking more havoc on the already crippled city. I am half a day behind on the other side of the world, but I am rattled to the core. I spend the morning fighting back tears, as I meet with the compassionate Digital Editors at the Bodleian to discuss text encoding and their work in progress.

By the end of the day, I have hatched a plan to relocate five hours south to Dunedin on my return to New Zealand, and complete my academic year with University of Canterbury remotely. Within a few days, I have gained approval from my research supervisors, which enables me to sufficiently gather my wits and attend to the last few days of the Oxford term.

Days of uninterrupted sunshine have become few and far between, and I spend much of the week indoors. I calm my jangled nerves with transcription, and an essay on eighteenth-century proposals for an English Academy. Impromptu pub summits and cafe conversations with other Canterbury students are frequent; commiserations for those most affected by the chaos at home are interspersed with farewells for those moving on to other universities.

On Friday night, I brave the pouring rain and make a run for it up the Broad and into the Sheldonian Theatre. Concert pianist Paul Lewis is performing Schubert, which promises to be an excellent way to appreciate the classically-inspired architecture of the University's principal assembly room. The hard seating is awful, and an apparently recent repaint disappointing, but the music is flawless, and worth the unpleasantness of aching joints and wet shoes.

The rain persists on Saturday, and I catch scenes of a rather soggy and drunken New College garden party from my tower room window. Trinity Term is the last of the Oxford academic year, and the summer holiday spirit is catching on despite the weather. I take in the half-empty glasses of Pimm's filling up with rain, and the croquet paraphernalia lying scattered and abandoned around Holywell Quad, as I ponder how to wrap up my last essay. I have enjoyed writing it, but I am enjoying finishing it even more, and looking forward to celebrating with hot chocolate and the Sunday paper at Patisserie Valerie.

WEEK 8

While my arguably more sensible friends are punting on the Cherwell, I am bunkered down in the English Faculty library, immersed in the online catalogue. With my final assignments submitted, I have time to start researching the use of crowdsourcing for digitising cultural heritage collections, which will be my focus for the rest of the academic year. Making the most of free access to Oxford resources in my last week, I am downloading research articles at a rate of knots, like a robber stuffing a sack full of loot. I have learned so much from my Oxford experience, but it is liberating to be in the driver's seat, compiling my own reading lists and choosing the direction of my work.

In my breaks, as I farewell my favourite places, I am still discovering. On my way back from Jericho, and an informal tour of Balliol, I find myself unexpectedly spellbound in the History of Science Museum, drawn in by the gleaming gilt brass of the sixteenth-century astrolabes. I have spent time in the grand and slightly imposing Ashmolean, which I experienced as a too-large cabinet of curiosities, and I'm intrigued as to why this relatively pint-sized museum, which I might have easily overlooked on the busy Broad, is so much more engaging. I suspect that it is something slightly intangible, related to the human scale of the building, the focus of the collection, and the number of objects on display, which makes a museum feel accessible or overwhelming.

On Tuesday evening, the Canterbury contingent converges on Rhodes House for a music recital-meets-talent show by Rhodes Scholars. We have been welcome here since the first reception to mark our arrival in April, and have returned for informal events throughout the term. Tonight's in-house entertainment begins in all seriousness with classical music at the grand piano, loosens up with a kind of world music medley, for which students have clearly raided the Music Faculty, moves on to a slick delivery of original rap (the unofficial winner), and ends with a hilarious flourish of amateur magic. As the boisterous ovation subsides, the doors are opened for a barbecue on the lawn.

In my tutorials on Wednesday, I commit the rooms to memory, appreciating for the last time the ample spaces for thinking that Oxford academics and students enjoy. At home, siphoned off the narrow corridors of tired buildings, Humanities academics are commonly squeezed into shoe-box offices lined with ugly steel shelving and aluminium windows. Here at New College, in a spacious study looking out to the green oval of the Great Quad, I sit opposite my tutor at a wide antique desk. Behind me, custom-fit wooden shelves perfectly accommodate various sizes of leatherbound books, some of which I have come to know intimately.

Today, we are both standing over the desk, studying several original manuscripts, discussing common trends in calligraphy and curious points of difference. I have covered so much ground in such a short time that my first star-struck conversation with him, when I shrunk at the question of "how is your Latin?", feels like a year ago. Now, we are chatty and comfortable, and I appear to have sufficiently proven myself worthy of his efforts. We cannot be far apart in age, and the atmosphere is almost collegial.

On the last night of Trinity Term, with my suitcase packed and bound for London, I spiral the tower stairwell, turn left at the New College gate, and stroll up the street to the Holywell Music Room. I have been invited to a Summer Concert by one of the performers — a Digital Editor at the Bodleian by day, chamber musician by night — which is a special way to experience what is claimed to be the oldest custom-built concert hall in Europe.

The eighteenth-century hall was restored in the 1960s, and the simplicity of the white room, with its modern arched windows and spare decor, is unexpected after weeks of historic grandeur. I am sitting in my usual spot for concerts, for a clear view of the stage — elevated in the dress circle, a few seats shy of centre — but for much of the evening my eyes are closed. I focus on the effects of notes drawn by thoughtful strings, and reflect on the precious gift of place and time that will forever be the highlight of my life. Everything that has come before has led me here. Everything that follows will be compared to this.

READING ALOUD

East sinks into the warm bath of voice, words tunnelling sonorous into bone. All too soon, she will be lulled unconscious and diverge from the path of story, but for now, she listens with eyes closed, transported. For today's reading, East lies outstretched in corpse pose, weak back aligned to the unforgiving futon, as West paces the room, lost to performance. The reader knows this story well, and so its world is quickly conjured, its characters given voice. His suburban monk-like cell, depressingly curtained to the too-bright of day, gives way to a fantastical, crumbling Gothic castle and its curiously named inhabitants.

West is tall and slightly stooped, with an awkward gait. He dresses plainly in clothes to which he pays no attention, and like East, is shaven headed. Temporarily dispelling his usual dark air of distrust and avoidance, West is a joyful reader and quietly commanding. It seems that only this room, in the sprawling, otherwise unoccupied house, is a safe space in which to expand and play. Today's enthusiasm is three-fold: a treasured text to introduce, revisit, and read aloud.

The novel's landscape is a welcome but not entirely effective distraction from the realities of this house, which East silently, disloyally, hates. Despite her efforts to imagine and inspire improvements, the extent of domestic neglect is frustrating and oppressive. Senseless though, to invest energy when neither landlord nor tenant has any interest in change; East is only a guest here.

The single-storey weatherboard bungalow, set back from a winding corner of the street, appears at the end of a narrow path overgrown with garden escapes. The view on approach is the single redeeming feature: an expanse of capital city and harbour from the generous hilltop perch. It is mystifying that only East seeks out this view from inside the house, claiming the lonely dining table as a researcher's desk.

Of the two dusty, deserted bedrooms, East follows the light, choosing to sleep with feet facing her home across the harbour. An old single mattress is dragged from the hallway, and clothes for two or three days at a time hang on hooks behind the door. The futon serves for talk and sex and films and readings, but only here, in a space staked out for solitude, can East sleep through the night.

On her third visit, there had been the question of the kitchen. The cupboards were filled with expired and rusting tins of beans, soup, fruit, the bottom drawer of the fridge frozen solid with an unidentifiable mass left by previous tenants. If East was going to stay here, the kitchen would need to be tackled. West's persistent diet of cereal, granny smith apples, white bread and peanut butter, which sat on the counter, would not suffice.

The further back East ventured into the property, the more menacing it became. Ancient black bags of rubbish and forgotten shoes blocked the doorway, which led sharply down, past the vine-strangled compost bins, to the unseen basement, green mould coating the walls like ivy. It is, however, important to be delicate. West is strangely attached to this house — the reader's own monastic *Gormenghast*.

It's disorienting to wake from reading-induced slumber in the middle of the day, and yet they know it's inevitable. East is always embarrassed to be pulled under so quickly, and annoyed to miss chunks of story that will not be retold, but this is the gift and curse of the reader. Today, the awkward moment is swiftly dismissed as West smiles, draws closer, talk stops, and they travel somewhere else together.

The intensity of their physical connection had been unexpected, like their pairing, after years of respecting rules of professional conduct and personal boundaries. For West, so long self-declared off limits to anyone, the first sparks of sex had been overwhelming. For East, despite a craving for smoothness, soft lines, a body that mirrored, the surrender to their powerful, spiritual undertow was otherworldly.

At first, their private talks, which had always been peppered with cleverness, laughter and delight, had moved outside their cramped, university office and across the water to a long stretch of wild coast, a hidden lake, a retired lighthouse. Their time no longer limited, conversation roamed wide and deep. Slowly, with care, they revealed their scars, and opened up new space to sit with each other.

There had been something about the late summer dream that reminded East of ghostly visitations in the night — the uncertainty of real or imagined. The sensation of lying, wrapped tightly from behind in West's arms, invoked such extraordinary pleasure. On waking, the desire for a physical relationship was a revelation. Compelled to fulfil what felt prophetic, East had sent a letter of love, and waited.

Lying together now, as their sweat cools and breathing slows, East's thoughts drift home. Like the house on the hill, it is sparsely furnished and offers few distractions for visitors. A folding card table and two metal stools for meals, a secondhand drafting table playing standing desk in the living room. A single mattress and stack of books on the floor in the bedroom. Intentional space, like the breathing room of wide margins on a written page.

East had moved there in the year of letting go, the year of questioning everything. Hair shorn, meat shun, weight shed, every hardened habit evaluated. Releasing the drag and drain of the city, East alighted on a small flat by the sea, happy to impose the distance of a ferry ride or a long, slow bus trip. Walking the bush before breakfast, working in a bikini and bare feet, letting the light in and sending it out, East glowed.

There had been nothing missing. West was not a salve for loneliness, or a banquet after a famine. In the space they had made, East had simply seen past, seen through, and was drawn to the cathedral of brilliance and suffering that West appeared to be. And so, riding the high of love, East is again willingly, wholeheartedly, bowing full to the needs of another.

West, who resents leaving this room, loathes the two bus trips around the bays, which East finds scenic and restful. The ferry too, for reasons difficult to articulate, is problematic, requiring West to travel with eyes tight shut past the small island that lies between them. Eager to smooth all edges, every few days East trades her house by the sea for West, and a darkened room in a gloomy house.

So much time spent travelling is becoming an obstacle, and East's doctoral thesis is suffering. Seemingly incapable of taking time to find middle ground, East declares that moving closer, back to the city, as soon as possible, is the solution. Within weeks, the house by the sea handed back, East is confined in a tiny room, in an ugly block of flats, in an old inner-city suburb. West is ecstatic: there is only a short walk between them.

The breakdown begins in the backseat, as they are driven around a peninsula that faces the hidden lake, the lighthouse. The stony beach where East danced steps around driftwood and plunged into the cold shock of sea. Her meditation room of black rock, licked smooth by the tide, and the ridge from which snow-capped peaks revealed themselves on a clear day. The shush of waves at night, the glorious native morning chorus.

Her torrent of tears cannot be contained, and the car is stopped for a feeble excuse: it's a nice day, we'll walk the rest of the way. East stumbles down to the beach, drops to the ground, digs shaking hands into the sand. She has sacrificed too much for love, and the sense of loss is so overwhelming that words cannot pass.

Their time together is limited now. There is no more reading aloud. East retreats, despairing, to unravel alone. The spell has broken, and the thought of returning to the house on the hill is appalling. They meet on a bench in a private corner of the Botanic Gardens, where East makes promises that will not hold water. They meet in a too-noisy cafe, where East fakes brightness while West sits shaking and hollow-eyed. They meet in a corridor of confusion, the signs of neurodivergence and mental illness in a language she does not yet understand. East will write the last page of their story, but West will end the book.

WRITING LESSONS

The three women take their seats around the small, low Formica table, like over-sized characters at a Wonderland tea party. The tallest takes the far corner, aligning her intimidating frame with the standard-issue steel bookshelf common to every academic's office on campus. Her soft-edged counterpart, at ease in her own space, settles in the centre of the room, in front of the ugly aluminium windows. With both of her supervisors facing the door, Alice is left with her back to it — a sitting duck for bad feng shui.

They have been playing out this scene every month for the past three years, shuffling marked-up sheets of white paper back and forth, watching Alice wrangle unnecessary riddles, and they ought to be finished by now. Her doctoral thesis — the weary Dormouse between them, struggling for respect — has become a source of awkwardness that makes these meetings unbearable.

Today, the blackness weighing down Alice is heavier than ever. For the first time in her life, she is going to be late, and she is furious. Missing the deadline for thesis completion means an end to her scholarship funding, and switching to the tiresome, drawn-out process of part-time study alongside full-time work. She has just turned forty, and she's been here long enough.

Dragging herself to the finish line in slow motion is not what she signed up for.

Three years ago, sitting front and centre in the induction seminar, listening attentively to a newly appointed Doctor of Philosophy caution the cohort about the high drop-out rate, Alice was certain that she would not become a pathetic statistic. Now, half-blinded by the glare of an overcast summer's day, and the exhausted patience of her supervisors, Alice is on the verge of telling them to stuff it.

Her reliable time management skills, and passion for her subject, are no match for the expectations of the most senior academic, whose work Alice finds difficult to read. Their opposing writing styles — the significance of which Alice has been downplaying for two years — are now quite clearly contributing to her delay. When the potential for creative conflict first became apparent, Alice chose loyalty to her teacher, employer, mentor, and champion over confrontation. Surely now, it was too late to request a replacement supervisor with a voice more attuned to her own.

Outside academia, Alice's writing is a tool for practical application, valued for its clarity and concision. In contrast to the conceptual labyrinths, complex syntax, and daunting vocabulary that characterises her supervisor's publications, Alice's work might be considered the output of an academic lightweight, but she has no interest in talking over people's heads. She has never, in fact, aspired to be an academic at all. The past three years of dedicated effort were intended to create knowledge of practical use, and make it freely available; now that she has done so, her thesis feels like superfluous paperwork.

If only she could finish a draft in peace, without these regularly scheduled intrusions and premature recommendations for revision over the tea table. Despite her secondary supervisor's encouragement to "just keep going", Alice feels obliged to respond to the lofty suggestions of the primary gatekeeper beneath whom, ultimately, her thesis must pass. Enjoyment of her daily writing practice is not a sufficient antidote for the menacing dance of one step forward, two steps back, like a puppet on a string, which is making Alice quite mad.

Never again will she subject her writing to such a crippling process. It won't be today, but one day soon, Alice will storm off in a sternly-worded blaze of black ink, and no-one in Wonderland will skip a beat. She will declare this whole shape-shifting pack of cards, which has served up as many frustrating blizzards as rewarding intellectual insights, a strange and haunting dream.

PIVOT

NORTH

The makeshift curtain pegged to the wire above the back window is no match for the streetlights of Thorndon; the jolly red, white and blue chequers glow hopelessly behind my head. The van rocks slightly with every passing car, and when the traffic eases around midnight, an early spring wind picks up, increasing the volume and thrash of giant evergreens either side of the gully. It feels like lying in the cabin of a boat, which isn't entirely unpleasant until I start to feel a little seasick. As camping spots go, I can do better, but my new sleeping bag is warm, the secondhand single mattress is more comfortable than the bed I've been sleeping on for months, and I'm thrilled to be on the giddy edge of a radical new way of life. Tonight is just a test run.

My recently purchased converted trade van is parked outside Wellington's Botanic Gardens, opposite the rented apartment I will soon vacate. Since paying for storage would undermine my commitment to the level of freedom I want to achieve, any possessions that don't fit in the van have been gifted to friends or exchanged with neighbours for pocket money. What little furniture the studio contains belongs to the landlord and won't be missed. It was only having to play favourites with my small collection of books that caused a twinge, but I didn't hesitate for long. I have always lived lightly, and letting go is all too easy. I've never considered that my continuous cycle of swapping one way of life for another might be a subversion of natural design.

The camper conversion is perfect for one, but leaves little room for sentiment. Most of my essentials — packed in sturdy, clear plastic containers — are stacked beneath the rough wooden frame of the bed. Clothes are rolled in small fabric boxes between the mattress and the window, and books, torch, and personal security alarm are close to hand. Tomorrow, the two kitchen cupboards by my feet will be filled with basic food supplies, a clutch of utensils, a small wooden board, and a single enamel plate, bowl, and cup.

Two weeks later, my alarm sings Monday from the soft box by my head, waking me before sunrise. I swap pyjamas for track pants and sweatshirt, tidy the bed, and peg the curtains back to reveal the calm of the morning. Clambering over to the front seat, I wind down the windows to let in the cool, salted air. I drive the van from my free camp in a quiet suburban cul-de-sac to the beach for breakfast.

A weekend pottering around Island Bay and Red Rocks reserve is about as close as I can get to the South Island without jumping in the tide and freestyling the rough Strait to the Sounds. Avoiding unwanted attention overnight, I steer clear of coastal car parks, free camping inconspicuously in a different residential street each evening. I have started a mental list of favourite spots (harbourside, sheltered, flat, quiet), to which I will randomly return until I have saved enough money to leave the capital city far behind.

Breakfast is muesli at the pop-up table between the front seat and the bed, as the kettle boils for coffee on the camping stove, and the fishing boats slosh the deep scoop of bay. The internal kitchen set up was a major drawcard, enabling me to stay warm and dry in inclement weather, and cook and eat in peace without the curious stares and comments of people passing by.

A childhood adventuring in Volkswagen Kombis has trained me to know good campervan design when I see it, but my budget could not stretch beyond a rusty, battered, white Toyota Hiace with acceptably high mileage. Small gas canisters fuel the portable two-ring stove, and running water is a ten-litre plastic jerry can turned upside down. A grocery list without meat or dairy has little need for a working fridge, and electric light is a luxury I can live without. I shower at work or the public pool. The laundry is a coin-operated machine wherever I can find one, and the toilet is a bucket with a lid in a pinch. As far as I'm concerned, the van is perfect for me, and I've already named it with affection and a custom sticker affixed to the back window: Pinot.

Accommodation aside, the day ahead is fairly typical white-collar screen slog. I scrape the used coffee grinds into my miniature rubbish bin, and give the plunger a quick rinse from the jerry can. Washing the dishes in a plastic basin is an awkward, tedious chore that can wait until the end of the day. Leaving the morning tide to ebb and flow beneath the gorse-covered hills without me, I cruise Pinot up the friendly, slightly shabby main street of the seaside suburb, past the settler villas and bungalows on the fringe, and through the inner city before peak-hour commuters slow the brief journey to a crawl.

Nearing the semi-circular hub and imposing cream colonnade of the Neo-Classical railway station, I park on the quay outside head office to shower and change into the conformist attire of a business analyst. At this hour, I will have the eleventh floor almost to myself. Stepping out of the lift into the quiet of the transparent landing, I pause to take in the impressive expanse of harbour that will soon dazzle with September sunlight from Petone to Pencarrow Head.

Before any of my colleagues have arrived, I am clean, dressed and out the door, backtracking to the other side of the central business district. I park Pinot on a rented slab of concrete, within walking distance of the website development company where I have been assigned, and join the flow of my project team through the door of the tired but once impressive glass building, in time for our first meeting of the day.

Inspired by the memoir of an American liberal arts student, who dodged debilitating college debt by free camping in a van, I had realised that the sooner I deleted rent from my budget, the faster I could finance my escape plan. Campervan life also made the dreary countdown to freedom more palatable, with the distraction of evenings and weekends outside the city, and fine-tuning tiny house living.

Plimmerton, Pukerua Bay, Martinborough, Stokes Valley, East Harbour. Calm, silent hours walking unpeopled coastlines, narrow tracks through native bush, and country lanes bright with spring. Sitting on the fringes with lighthouses and islands, beachcombing for unusual beauty, reading novels on rainy weekends, waiting. By October, I have paid off my overloaded credit card and loan for the van, and saved enough for a one-way ferry ticket to Picton. Assuming everything went according to plan, by the end of November I would have enough to tide me over for a few weeks on a shoestring, until I secured a very different job.

I'm a member of a large team dedicated to designing the national census, which was fascinating at first. This morning, sitting at a long, shared desk in the draining glow of a screen, bored without enough work to do despite requests for more, I'm considering my options.

I want to work at something with my hands, which doesn't involve a keyboard, and won't tie me down for too long. Something that quiets the mind, outside perhaps, work connected to the land. An employer who won't ask why I abandoned a PhD so close to the finish line, and the foundations of a career I have clearly worked hard to build. A winery, a restaurant, fruit picking?

At lunch time I grab an apple from the complimentary fruit bowl and join the friendly crowd around the communal kitchen table. A group of software developers are messing about with foosball until their pizza order arrives. The testers are lounging on bean bags with two-minute noodles in the sunny corner of the room next door. A new recruit is manning the almost continuous crunch and grind of the industrial espresso machine. I like the vibe and almost fit in, but my role here is temporary, and I'm more a guest than one of the gang. They include me in the conversation, but I keep the details of my plans to myself, avoiding the inevitable jokes about mid-life crisis.

Two weeks before my last day at the office, I am alternating library books with window-framed impressions of Eastbourne through torrential rain. It is extreme but somewhat fitting weather to farewell the rugged, windswept peripheral place that I once called home. From my cushioned reading position in the corner of the passenger seat, *The Man Who Quit Money* splayed open in my lap, I watch the blurred hunks and splinters of driftwood clattering in and out from the stony shores. Zipping up a red puffer jacket to keep out the draft, I'm trying to ignore the tired window seals, which are struggling to keep the van watertight in these conditions.

On Sunday evening, I take the scenic route to the opposite

side of the harbour, winding around the bush-clad hills of the Eastern bays for the last time. Passing the storm-spattered Mansfield cottage, a deserted Petone Beach, and the inner-city waterfront, I finally reach the confident jut of Miramar Peninsula — a short but scenic drive from the office.

On a quiet residential street, in the middle of the night, I wake in panic to the van being rocked violently from side to side. In my disorientation, I'm not sure if I'm awake or dreaming. Recently, I have been spooked by some guys hanging around on the footpath outside as the sporadic boom and crackle of annual fireworks lit up the sky overhead. Tonight, it feels like people are trying to tip the van over.

As the rocking subsides, and my mind clears and sharpens, I finally register: earthquake. I have never been in a vehicle during a strong quake before, and my usually fine-tuned instinct for magnitude has been thrown off. I'm going to need information, but my laptop is stowed in my locked office cabinet, and my cheap mobile phone is just a phone. Without the internet, my only option is the van's radio, which I have never used. I pull on some extra layers for warmth, and climb over to the front passenger seat. Fiddling with the dials through oblivious pop music and useless static, I find the monotone of a news reader, describing a massive 7.8 near the top of the South Island. Anyone near the coast is instructed to move to higher ground.

I'm not the only one listening to the tsunami warning. Cars start streaming onto the street from the houses around me, heading away from the harbour lapping close to Marine Parade only metres away. Bleary eyed and heart pounding, I lurch about, opening the curtains and securing loose objects before turning the van around. More familiar with the coast than the city heights, I have no idea where I'm headed, but the evacuation is jamming the streets so I'm not going anywhere fast.

Eventually the neighbourly crawl starts to climb, and I follow the pack stop-start up the closest hill. The narrow, winding street is nerve-racking in the dark, and I park as soon as I can see the city lights far below. My bed is sloped on an awkward angle, and there are people outside talking, but I'm grateful to return to my sleeping bag. Curled into a ball on my side, I imagine lying on my back in shavasana, and hear some tension release with a faint crack in my spine as I count slowly: one, two, three, four.

After a long night riding the tremors, drifting in and out of an anxious doze, I'm relieved to give up on sleep with the sound of the alarm, but the uncertainty of the day ahead is unnerving. I brush fingers through my short hair, and dress awkwardly in the gloomy slant of the van, before unveiling the vague surroundings behind the curtains. From what I can see, the street is quiet, but for a couple of neighbours chatting by a letterbox on the opposite side. Behind them, the impressive city sprawl gives me a jolt — I am much higher than I had realised.

I don't yet know the extent of the quake damage, or where it's safe to go, and a clammy sense of isolation starts to seep into the void of my morning routine. I belatedly send a few brief messages to family and friends outside the city to assure them of my safety, and explain that I will phone when I can recharge the battery, which is running low. I haven't listened to any news since the tsunami warning, but now, sitting cross-legged on the passenger seat, I stare vacantly out the window as I absorb the latest reports of devastation and disruption from Kaikoura to Wellington.

The descriptions are spare, but I can picture it all too easily. Landslides and wrecked bridges. Damaged docks, ferries suspended. People stranded and supplies cut off as railway, roads and highways are closed. Sewage systems compromised, water restricted. Schools and universities closed. Buildings cracked or collapsed, windows smashed, power out. People in the capital are to avoid the central city until further assessments can be made. Feeling sickened and hollow, I have been here before.

Desperate to get down from the heights and put the awful night behind me, I can at least move to a more calming location now the East Coast has seen the worst. Navigating the van with care, I descend to a peaceful, tree-lined street a cautious distance from the beach, where I park outside the well-tended garden of a grey and white bungalow to await my employer's instructions. As my coffee brews dark and strong on the kitchen table, the roof starts to drum gently with rain.

Monday, Tuesday, Wednesday. Dreary days passed in an anxious state of limbo, punctuated only by a text message each evening instructing me to stay away from the office. With only a few days left before my contract ends, it looks like I may not be going back to work at all. As shops on the city fringe reopen, I replace the charger locked in my off-limits office, and bring my phone back to life. I find a grimy internet cafe for backpackers, and check in with my colleagues using a keyboard so worn that letters are missing. Most people are occupied with children, a few are attempting to work from home. It's a relief to be connected, but now I have a new concern.

By Thursday, relentless, torrential rain is leaking through the window seals and trickling down the walls of the van, into my clothes and bedding. The pressure-cooker of my distress ramps up. Skirting the crippled chaos of the CBD, I move to the depressing but familiar concrete shelter of a supermarket car park in Thorndon to think. Boiling the kettle for tea, I watch the constant flow of people, in with arms empty, out with arms full, going about their comparatively normal lives.

What I need is somewhere safe and dry for a couple of days to empty the van and salvage my gear. I have to get out of the city, far away from the aftershocks and merciless weather, and I need to do it today. With the South Island ferries out of action, and radio reports of slips and road closures, there is a very real possibility of the main route out being completely cut off. The only option I can see is to drive in the opposite direction that I want to go. I phone my manager to put my resignation into effect immediately, inform family in Auckland of my imminent arrival, and cut myself loose.

My relief — to be moving, leaving, taking control — is palpable and instantaneous. Within minutes, I'm on the motorway in high gear, passing over the hampered railway lines and empty ferry terminals, tracing the last strip of coast before turning inland between the dark hills and heading north. I will return when I can cross the Strait, making for a strange sort of unprepared, half goodbye to my home of five years.

Passing over the invisible city boundary, I slow to navigate suburban flooding, splashing nervously through a series of swimming pool roundabouts, as I crawl with so many others along the muddy chop of Kapiti Coast. Impatient at the thought of the nine-hour drive ahead, I urge the traffic to pick up the pace, talking to no one. Turning on the radio to pass the time, I listen astonished to the local news: the road I took out of Wellington has just been closed behind me.

I drive up the centre of the island through the night, stopping only for toilets and fuel. Without my usual appetite for scenery and nostalgia, favourite picnic spots pass by in a blur of determination. As darkness descends around Lake Taupo, I wind down the windows for the scent of pine forest on the crisp night air. An hour south of my destination — the last breath of country before I hit city sprawl — I pass the town and cemetery of my grandparents, and whisper a loving hello.

Around two in the morning, I exit the Northern motorway and guide the van through the sleeping North Shore suburbs to Castor Bay. Not wanting to wake my family in the middle of the night, I drive past the house and down the hill. I wrap my frayed nerves in the solace of the small cove, and doze in my clothes until it's light enough to swim.

SOUTH

The dark belly of the ferry rumbles with vehicles waiting to be released at Picton into the sunshine of the December afternoon. Among the passengers lulled by the turquoise cruise through the majestic Sounds, I sit patiently at the wheel, watching for the signal to move forward. The dust on the dashboard judders, the front window needs a clean. The smell of petrol through the vent takes me back to childhood, recalling memories of other vans, other ferry crossings, the comforting density of homemade hot cross buns as we queued for the English Channel at Easter. I get the nod and raised hand from a burly man in a beanie, and start my new life with the clang of a gangplank.

Before the quake, I had intended to amble and gypsy, to pass the summer with an easy zigzag drive south to Central Otago. I had no specific destination, no fixed plan, except a landscape that clears my mind and lifts my soul, and for life to be different. Now, my route out of aftershock territory is dictated and direct. The main state highway down the East Coast is closed, and alternate routes are plagued by the traffic of emergency services and supply vehicles. To circumvent the chaos, I must take an unfamiliar western route down the island, and I need to step on it if I want to outrun the teeming rain forecast for my direction. I've done my best to reseal the windows, but I'm in no hurry to test my efforts in a region infamous for wet weather.

Despite the circumstances, I'm determined to savour my first moments back on the mainland, and for now, the weather is on my side. Windows down, right elbow out, I follow the trail of ferry traffic through the funnel of forested hills and along the river to Blenheim. A glimpse of peak and late snow up ahead is enough to make me cheer with joy. I am not southern born, but this is a homecoming.

Blenheim is quiet with the damaged main street closed off, and I would prefer to pass right through, but I want to shower before I head inland into open country. I negotiate the déjà vu of orange traffic cones, emergency tape, and detour signs in the direction of the public pool, which, thankfully, is open.

Walking into a large concrete structure in unstable territory sets off my internal alarm, but I know the impressive new facility will be code compliant. Designed to embrace natural light, the architecture is a pleasant distraction from my knotted stomach and hollow legs. In the pristine, softly lit changing rooms, a dinner-plate power shower blasts me clean of road dust, sea salt and anxious sweat, before I succumb to the temptation of the glassy swim lanes and release the pockets of muscle tension into my wake.

As the sunrise sneaks in around the edges of the curtains the next morning, I take a moment to orient my resting place in the stillness. South Island. Wairau Valley. Verge off the main road. Apple tree by the fence. Right. Inside the sleeping bag I am warm as toast, but the tip of my nose betrays the dew on the grass outside — I'll need to layer up. Changing quickly, I straighten the bedding, clip back the curtains, and pull the heavy side door open to take in my surroundings while I make breakfast.

With no people or buildings in sight, I have, it seems, left it all behind, and as of this morning, my life is starting to make sense. I have followed the river through wine country to the heart of the island, reassured by the dark green, muscular bulk and sweep of the hills either side. The winding road ahead will take me through small, pinprick towns to the West Coast, where I will dodge tourist traps on the wild and moody route south, recalled only vaguely from a school holiday trip decades ago. I estimate two days from here to the dry calm of Central; I can come back and play tourist myself another time.

I fill my thermos with tea for the drive, and slather two pieces of bread with peanut butter and jam for later. I rinse the dishes outside on the grass, and settle them in the plastic basin with a tea towel so they don't rattle. As I stow the table away, my lower back twinges with the tenacious hangover of cumulative injury. Long days sitting in a worn front seat, driving a clunky manual, are doing my body no favours.

The rain hits sideways at Haast the next day, just as I take the bend at the river mouth, heading inland to the low mountain pass across the Southern Alps. I whoop with victorious relief at my near escape: I'm less than two hours from Central. The shift in weather fogs the van windows within minutes, forcing me to inch one down for fresh air, but as I enter the misty, rain-spangled beech forest, I'm rewarded with the hypnotic pummel of waterfall song.

The effect of the pass is so intoxicating that I'm disoriented when I arrive on the other side sooner than anticipated. Having crossed the invisible border between two regions, I find myself cruising, enchanted, through a small riverside community. When the rain stops and the clouds break at the top of a lake I don't immediately recognise, it's more appealing to sustain wonder and continue driving than stop and check the map.

The scene is fantastical, sublime. Great, god-like shafts of sunlight glint the peaks, skim the surface of the water and the flanks of awesome, mountainous gatekeepers. I don't know exactly where I am, but I tearfully vow to always live within reach of this place, to never leave the South Island again. When the road veers east to cross an isthmus, I stop at a lookout to get my bearings and understand: Lake Hawea ahead, Lake Wanaka behind.

I carry on down between the two kissing lakes to the bustling Wanaka township, where I refuel, buy groceries, and park for the night to regroup. I have reached my general destination intact, but only just. I tell myself that the rattle I can hear coming from the van is only loose gravel around the wheels, collected while driving through numerous road works since Auckland. The small stones I could spy from an awkward crouch in the supermarket car park I've swept free, but the persistent clatter is disconcerting. Curtailed by circumstance, my savings are slim, and the prospect of denting what little I have with a mechanic's bill is one that I'm not, for now, willing to entertain.

I need a job, but seasonal work doesn't kick into high gear for several weeks, and right now, I can barely hoist myself out of the driver's seat. My romantic notion of long days spent harvesting and pruning vineyards and orchards has evaporated in the face of a low wall of pain from hip to hip, and the reality of a middle-aged back prone to twinge and lock to a standstill. Applications sent ahead from Auckland to southern wineries for back-office jobs have come to nothing.

Somewhere between Haast and Hawea, a vague dream of working as a cook took hold of my imagination, buoying me with the rush of reinvention. Now, as the sun sets over Dublin

Bay, catching the play of dust motes in the front cabin, I comb the columns of the *Cromwell Bulletin* for job listings, and prepare to pitch my outdated hospitality credentials. I leave phone messages for restaurant managers in Clyde and Arrowtown, before pulling the curtains across what feels like my first night home.

CENTRAL

The 1950s roughcast bungalow could be mistaken for the same house, but I know better. Ten years earlier, lying in the shaded hammock stretched between two poles of the veranda, I could see across the meadows to the shimmer of Lake Dunstan. Gardens, bursting unashamedly with an abundance of roses and peonies, surrounded the house, which sat at once humble and proud as the neighbour to a pioneer family estate. It was here near Lowburn, visiting my aunt, that I first fell in love with Central, and the sadness the house carries now almost overwhelms me.

Hemmed in tight by new black fences and kitset cul-de-sacs, the house has been readdressed and effectively turned around on paper to suit the plans of a sprawling new residential development. The back door is now the front, making the house look somewhat embarrassed. A new driveway carves up a tiny, tinder-dry lawn from a new street. The garden has been pulled out, the peonies are gone. The heritage apricot tree, picked for jam that gleamed in the pantry, jars gemstone bright, has been replaced by a neighbouring garage. If there was still a hammock, it would look across a concrete car park to the beige backside of a two-storey, Lego-block resort on the obscured lake, which is, by some epic feat of extravagant engineering, closer than it was before.

Her home as I knew it is gone, and this is no place to linger. I am thankful that she decamped before the bulldozers arrived, and I am not obliged to visit, although I will pass this way many times. I carry on down the highway to a stretch of unspoiled lakefront, to cool my ankles in the clear water, and wash my memory clean.

Less than an hour away, Arrowtown too has changed, but here I'm curious to explore. The quaint, weatherboard, settler cottages lining the streets to the small town are fascinating as ever, but seem to have perked up with the recent activity. The deciduous trees overhead, which make for a dazzling display each autumn, offer lush respite from the midday sun. Since I last walked the tired main street, numerous trendy eateries, wine stores, and up-market shops have taken up residence in its historic buildings. The nineteenth-century gold mining hub is buzzing.

When the lunch rush has passed, I hover outside the jar-lined windows of the old-fashioned sweet shop. I study the Neapolitan cafe and restaurant opposite, where I've been asked to hand deliver my résumé. The wooden building is painted the warm colours of earth, the swinging sign is plain and unassuming. Beyond the deep shade of the corrugated iron veranda, traditional ingredients fill the low bay window on one side, bentwood chairs and small tables on the other. The place appears welcoming, authentic, and has the distinctive air of a family business, which it is. I take a deep breath and cross the street, doing my best to appear calm and confident as I walk through the double wooden doors.

It has been almost twenty years since I worked an industrial kitchen, so this is a long shot. Conjuring a viable résumé has been a test of memory, and an exercise in curation rather than chronology; the resulting one-pager highlights basic culinary skills and willingness to learn over currency. Beyond my ability to make a good first impression, I'm relying on an employer being as desperate for staff in high season as I am to start work.

I wait by a half-empty cabinet of pastries until the handsome Italian owner farewells a customer. When he greets me, I'm prepared to sit and chat, but the exchange is brief and non-committal. He will read my résumé and be in touch in a few days. He seems less interested than he was on the phone — perhaps he has someone in mind for the job already. With time to kill before my interview in Clyde tomorrow, and the sounds from the van becoming more of a concern, I steel myself for the prognosis of a mechanic, and backtrack to the neighbouring service town of Alexandra.

The van hugs the rock face as I wind cautiously through the narrow Kawarau Gorge, taking care not to veer across the lane with the distraction of stunning views. On the other side, Chard Farm vines blanket the precarious foothills, watched over by Tuscan-inspired architecture the colour of rosé. I mirror the farm road to the river crossing, where tourists are paying to throw themselves off an adjacent bridge, in a spirit of thrill and entertainment.

Reaching the flat straight of the Gibbston road, my shoulders drop, my pulse calms. I slow down a little to enjoy the picture postcard of each distinctive winery against its dramatic backdrop, pulling over to let impatient drivers pass by. The old and the new estates take care to honour the landscape: there is no glitz or flashing signage here. Peregrine's elegant cellar canopy, evoking a falcon taking flight from the valley floor, always makes me smile.

At Nevis Bluff the road narrows again, squeezing me through the hook, and around the loop like the taught thread of a sewing machine. The glacial blue, hydroelectric rush of Roaring Meg fills my ears, and I spy the remnants of a gold-mining shanty town, huddled low against the harsh slopes of schist and scree. Soon, I'm out the other side in the big wide open, zipping through stone fruit orchards and roadside stalls.

I'm tempted to stop and rest on the cool lawn of the

Cromwell historic precinct, but I need to reach the workshop before it closes for the day. Skirting the town, I stick to the highway and head for the Clutha River crossing, stealing a glimpse up the lake back to Lowburn. At Deadman's Point, I take the turn and accelerate along the smooth, wide road of the gorge, past the ruby mass of spur valerian on the bank, and sturdy pastel totems of lupin. I don't stop at the lookout or the gold miners' plaque. I leave the dry tufts of wild thyme at Champagne Gully to be picked another day. Topping the ridge, I pass by the turn off to Clyde, and hurtle down the other side into Alex.

The mechanic's face is grim with the verdict as he crosses the concrete forecourt to where I'm waiting in the shade. He has the look of a concerned father, knowing the routes I've taken in the van, with a cam belt about to snap. At any moment, the engine could seize up, I could lose control of the steering, the brakes could fail. I listen, wide-eyed and gut-twisted, as he outlines what needs to be done without delay. It's going to cost me a small fortune to fix, but I'm lucky to have avoided catastrophe. It's going to take time, for parts and labour. The mechanic arranges a courtesy car, which has seen better days itself, so I can get to Clyde for my interview. He kindly agrees to me staying in the van overnight outside the workshop, until it's good to go.

The following afternoon, in the street-facing bar of a restaurant in Clyde, I'm settled on a plush sofa, upright and genial, résumé balanced in my lap. The interior of the old building is all wood, schist, worn brick and soft lighting, and as I sit beneath the heavy beams, surrounded by framed sepia photos, I feel right at home.

An intense, burly, apron-clad chef, slightly younger than

me, is perched impatiently on the edge of the armchair to my right. As he stares outside at nothing in particular, I focus on the short, plain, no-nonsense woman in her sixties, dwarfed by the armchair opposite. In appearance and manner, she reminds me of a former employer, who I would rather not recall; her thin veil of civility suggests potential for unpleasantness. As hands-on manager, she is outlining the full-time position they need to fill as soon as possible, and takes my measure as she speaks.

They need a competent cook for the establishment's cafe, and, reading between the lines, appear willing to overlook my lack of certifications and recent experience if I'm willing to overlook minimum wage. I respond with wholehearted enthusiasm, eloquently making my case that I'm the right person for the job. I deflect their queries about my white-collar orientation, assuring them I'm fully committed to a career change. Maintaining eye contact, I explain that I'm looking for a chance to prove myself, at which point I finally get the chef's attention.

Two hours later, I am ambling along the narrow river trail between Alex and Clyde, brushing dry, waist-high grass with my outstretched hands, tranquillising my nervous energy. The restaurant in Arrowtown has just turned me down, and the only other vacancies are in the hectic hustle of Queenstown an hour away. I have no family or friends in Central, but that has never influenced the places I've chosen to call home; for now, right here is where I want to stay.

I've stopped to appreciate a warm yellow patch of Californian poppies at my feet when the phone rings. I haven't met the owner of the restaurant in Clyde, but she tells me now that I've made quite an impression on her staff. Can I start in two days? Absolutely. I arrange a short-term loan with family to help tide me over until pay day, and head back to Alex for a library card.

The weighted steel handle is chill and comfortable in my small right hand, the long, slim, Japanese blade flashing clean and uncompromising in the hospitality showroom lights. The all-purpose cook's knife is almost top of the range and more than I can comfortably afford, but it's the bare minimum I can get away with. In the impulsivity of my career change, I had overlooked some basic requirements, and the manager's scathing remarks, when I turned up last week empty handed, have left me no choice. By the time I've piled the cased knife, a low-end sharpener, and two blue cotton butcher's aprons on the industry supply store counter, I'm broke.

Mercifully, traditional chef whites are not compulsory for my position, although I can imagine the withering comments behind my back from the disdainful expressions of my colleagues. I arrive at seven in the morning, five days a week, in black canvas shoes, a branded t-shirt, and black cotton drawstring pants bought months ago with fruit picking in mind. Alongside a colleague, I cook breakfasts in the luxurious expanse of the open kitchen of the restaurant, for customers seated in the adjoining cafe. Before the chefs arrive to prep for dinner, we clean and switch to the small back kitchen for the remainder of our shift, where I feel more relaxed, despite the crush.

The morning after my supply splurge, I kit up in the restaurant's tiny laundry room, already hot with the rumbling dryer. I proudly don my new blue apron, circling my waist once around the back, and tying tight at the front. I loop a clean white tea towel over the ties at my left-hand side, enjoying an old ritual. Feeling redefined and purposeful, I enter the back door of the kitchen, side-stepping the unfriendly, flour-dusted baker, and set up my station in a rectangle of cool, pristine, stainless steel. An hour later, hovering beside me as I rinse my new knife at the sink, the manager scornfully observes that the chefs consider my chosen brand unworthy, and doesn't bat an eyelid when I point out that she has the same one.

After years of academic work that became mired in unpalatable complication, using my hands to swiftly create simple things for a simple purpose is a gift. My head empties of everything that is not right in front of me, not relevant to this moment. I orbit around ingredients, industrial ovens, and naked flame, tending to toasting muesli, roasting tomatoes, poaching eggs. I promptly dispatch sweet slices, hand-high cakes. In the kitchen I am fully present, focused, efficient, and happily required to speak little. Despite the daily snark and unnecessary micro-management from the boss, I know that I am doing good work, holding my own. I'm considered an outsider, but as the days pass and I prove myself a reliable member of the team, the frosty atmosphere around me begins to thaw.

In the dry heat of December, shifts are hot work, but breaks are discouraged by the manager, who doesn't take them herself. At most, I grab five minutes outside on a slab of schist by the kitchen door — chairs being intentionally absent. By the afternoon, I'm physically spent. I could shower at the pool in Alex, and use the laundromat in town, but after my first few days, I'm ready for a base where I can conserve my limited energy.

Of the three campgrounds on offer, I choose the one with the most shade and distance from the road, and organise a weekly rate for an unpowered site. Slowly navigating the ruts up a gentle rise nicknamed Lavender Hill, I park where I can lie in bed and look through the front window to the vast mountainous spread of Old Man Range. Behind me, a slope of pine trees provides shelter, and at the far end of the section, I can take in the scenery from the icy shallows of the children's pool.

Until the plots fill with the cheerful din of school holiday campers, the communal facilities hum quietly with the assorted languages of seasonal workers, who nod in recognition as we bookend each day with coffee making and dish washing.

Hoovering up cafe leftovers at the end of each shift, I rarely need to cook dinner, leaving me free to read, write, and visit the river.

Propped against a ragged hill of barren rock, Alexandra's giant illuminated clock is an iconic feature of the town, but I am drawn to the elegant nineteenth-century suspension bridge below. The old wooden planks shudder and creak as I cross the short stretch of river that serves in summer as a swimming hole, delivering me onto the dusty road of Graveyard Gully at the foot of a vineyard.

Turning right, my back to the trendy new homes popping up like clay-coloured mushrooms along the river, I follow the winding, unsealed road past the apricot orchards, perfuming the route with a dry sprig of wild thyme crushed between my fingers. Tonight, the evening is warm, hushed, and still. Wild flowers greet me at every turn, but I pass no one.

Where two rivers converge, the road veers inland, petering out at the remnants of a pioneer resting place, almost lost to the passage of time since the gold rush. I pause outside the old stone wall of the cemetery, imagining the tent township that once was. I contemplate the resilience of those who sailed from the other side of the world to the unknown, who struggled through snowstorms and baking summers to establish themselves here. The physical challenges of my toil are pathetic in comparison.

Working on my feet all day, and standing for extended periods at the same workstation, has ratcheted the pain in my hips and lower back to daily reliance on heavy-duty painkillers. The repetitive strain of chopping, slicing and dicing soon impairs my right hand, dragging pain to my elbow, and then my shoulder. Time off between shifts becomes dedicated to rest and recovery, but it's never long enough, and within a fortnight I'm starting to question the sustainability of my latest professional reinvention.

I keep my difficulties to myself, avoiding the ridicule that would likely follow, but chronic pain is impacting my patience. As each day passes, it becomes more difficult to tolerate a manager who has revealed herself to be a shameless bully. Having thrown all manner of darts at me, she has discovered that I'm not such an easy mark, but when a polite and kind-hearted new recruit in her late teens proves to be the ideal punching bag, my hard-wired instinct to battle injustice rears up.

I avoid direct confrontation through the busy lead up to Christmas, but by New Year's Eve, the combination of toxic atmosphere and physical pain becomes too much. I hand in my resignation, complete with a concise, professional critique of management style that surprisingly gains her belated respect. Within a month of starting the job, I'm gone.

DUNEDIN

Temporarily crippled, emotionally defeated, and unemployed with no Plan B, I default to putting geographical distance between myself and the site of failure for a fresh start. I head east in the direction of the coast and a friendly face, arriving in the city of Dunedin the following day. Not wanting to disclose my desperation by landing on a friend's doorstep in tears, I check in to a leafy campground close by, and spend the weekend trying to pull myself together. I'm feeling so helpless that I've lost my appetite for fearless free camping.

Now, I can finally follow doctor's advice and allow my body complete rest, but my bank balance doesn't stretch to the specialist treatment recommended for my recurring joint pain. With nothing to do but try and envisage my future, the grievous loss of professional identity, associated with PhD withdrawal and career desertion, starts to seep under the high walls of my remorselessness. It will be another year before I admit deep regret at abandoning my thesis in the face of overpowering emotions, but for now, proven ill-suited to physical work at the age of forty, it's time to accept that I'm destined for a desk job. Lying on the grassy riverbank, as my fellow campers clatter in and out of the shared kitchen, I sadly relinquish the balm of big sky country, and resign myself to the professional opportunities that the city has to offer. There is no turning back.

By Monday night, I'm living in a 1930s brick bungalow, perched high on the sunny side of a neighbouring valley. I'm installed in the spare bedroom of an old friend, who had pragmatically suggested that if I was prepared to spend money on a camping ground, I may as well give it to her for art supplies. I'm grateful for her amusing company and moral support, and a semblance of routine that would usually provide much-needed emotional stability, but I am so engulfed in darkness that I'm struggling to get out of bed each day.

To see my tiny home and associated freedom parked pathetically in a suburban backyard is disheartening, and made worse by the fact that the van has failed its warrant of fitness and is now illegal to drive. Tending to the necessary repairs would be throwing good money after bad, and I can't afford them anyway.

The university is the city's largest employer, but I feel sick at the thought of working in an environment that will constantly remind me of academic failure, and my timing couldn't be worse. A controversial restructure that involves culling hundreds of jobs is underway, and my numerous applications don't get me as far as an interview for even the lowliest part-time administrative position.

Encouraged by my stalwart friend, I branch out, applying to any role in the city that even vaguely aligns with my credentials and experience, but as another week passes unfruitfully my funds dry up, and I'm at the bottom of the barrel. I can't bring myself to ask family for another loan. I was raised to stand on my own two feet, and have been working since the age of eleven; I don't borrow money lightly. Sitting in the garden-filtered light, at the old wooden desk squeezed into my bedroom, it occurs to me with incredulity that for the first time in my life I might be eligible for the dole.

I sternly inform my horrified ego that decades as a taxpayer make me as entitled to apply as anyone else in a time of need, but jumping through the numerous hoops for government job-seeker support requires more determination and humility than I can summon. An expert form-filler, I can stomach the tiresome paperwork, but when I learn that it's mandatory to attend a series of job-seeker workshops, despite having secured twenty jobs to date, I balk and throw in the towel.

The jobs I'm best suited for are in the cities, and until remote working becomes mainstream, I need to show up in person. Dunedin is ruling itself out, and I'm too quake-rattled to return to Christchurch. Opportunities in smaller South Island cities are thin on the ground, and would probably paint me into a more restrictive corner. Backtracking to Wellington — the scene of my professional suicide — is a no-go. Somewhere, half-buried beneath my cauldron of emotional chaos, I'm aware that living close to family right now might be a good thing. I steel myself for the last resort: applying for work amidst the high-rises and gridlocked traffic of Auckland.

NORTH

As soon as I widen my job search, I find it: the rarest of dream jobs. Boosted is New Zealand's crowdfunding platform for the arts, and it needs an Operations Manager and website overhaul. Over the past five years, I have become one of the country's leading experts in non-profit crowdsourcing, and designing websites for this purpose. The job promises professional redemption, and I can't write the application fast enough. My cover letter assures decision makers at the Arts Foundation that I will be in Auckland within the next week, and available for interview.

I can't afford to repair the van, and I don't want to leave it in my friend's driveway. Unable to imagine any scenario in which I return for it, and desperate for cash, I sell my dear little home for parts to a car wrecker on the far side of town. I book a one-way flight to Auckland, and fill two cheap, jumbo-sized suitcases with my possessions. After only two weeks in Dunedin, I'm gone.

The smooth concrete warms my soles as I walk barefoot in small, contemplative circles at the top of a steep driveway, looking across the harbour to the friendly volcanic island of my childhood. I've been on the phone with Boosted's General Manager for over an hour. We're both so galvanized by the electric back-and-forth of this interview that we don't want to stop talking. I'm fairly confident that the job is mine for the taking, but this is the first in a three-step process; I will be required to meet members of the team, and demonstrate that I'm a good fit for the organisational culture.

By the following week, I've passed the tests (thanks in part to my street cred as a poet), secured the position, and reinvented myself yet again. Typically, my father declares that it was all "meant to be", but I believe that I have simply made the best of another bad situation. It will take months to financially recover from my latest "adventure", but I'm relieved to have the means to do so.

My pivot to a nomadic lifestyle will be reframed loosely as a "sabbatical" spared of the details — a throwaway line at networking events. My pivot from academia will be reframed as a strategic career move. For now, at least, I have a reason to hold my head high. I have sacrificed my beloved Otago, but I console myself with the summertime bath of ocean at the bottom of the hill, and the white sand of a small cove between my toes.

BAD WEATHER

BLANK CANVAS

Leaning back in my white wicker chair, I consider the canvas on the tall wooden easel. A clear southern sky in block colour blue, a bold alpine line slicing the horizon. The balance and simplicity are pleasing — minimalist but evocative. Too simple? When I first began painting in my exacting twenties, I would take my finished canvases off the wall, and edit them mercilessly. Is knowing when to stop a talent you are born with or a skill you can learn?

After a year of city-trapped longing, the first unexpected glimpse of the Southern Alps from this weatherboard square, rented unseen, had taken my breath away; I'm trying to distil that moment. Later, I'll be satisfied that I continued painting, but my eye will always be drawn to the bottom-right corner, where an attempt to improve went awry. More inclined in middle age to accept Done over Perfect, I will hang 'Joy' above the fireplace, delighted to have a mountain in my living room.

This afternoon, the studio is bursting with sunshine like a glasshouse, the open door inviting scents of rosemary and lavender. Surrounded by windows and garden, I'm immersed in green, waiting for my rose tea to brew black. I observe the foxing on the back of my palms, how much they have aged since space and light last inspired me to pick up a paintbrush.

Silent, orderly friends keep me company: jam jar bouquets of generous powderpuff sweepers, sensible all-purpose mediums, fine fan brushes, and whispers of white. The smallest palette knives rest in the deep blue of my apron pocket. Towers of acrylic paint pots contain perfect circles of poetic colour: Japanese Laurel, Midnight Moss, Pelorus, Parchment. The drop cloth beneath my feet is the striped green and white of the Edwardian punting sheds an hour's drive north. A few streets away, Little Ben strikes the quarter hour — the surprising, dignified sound of an English town from the heartland of New Zealand.

I arrived here three weeks ago, alone in the dark after a three-day drive down the North Island to the South. I am starting again (again), knowing no-one. Taking up my tools, drawing together slivers of connection and community, forging a small space for myself on the periphery. My touchpoints are the swimming pool and the library. I live in a triangle.

North facing, at the midway point of a long stretch of insignificant road, my rented house sits squared to the tracks and low to the mid-Canterbury plains. Behind the section squats the threat of intrusive, thumping rhythm from the neighbour's garage. Long nights of crate clinking, and irritating, oafish laughter convert to overflowing recycle bins by morning. From the corner of my eye, I regularly assess the potential for disruption, unacknowledged. I'm becoming the peevish old woman next door, irrelevant.

After a year of shuttling from guest room to shared flat to a dim but private basement by the sea, this tired, creaking bungalow is a castle, a place in which I feel instantly taller, stronger. I have space, a garden, things to tend. I am breathing deep, releasing a circus of thought, pushing pause on a tumble dryer of worry. I seek *slow*, I seek *still*, I want so much to *stay*. I walk the boundaries of my modest estate, head tilted back to the sky, or cocked to appreciate the roses. The late summer standards are so heavily laden they are leaning. I count them, ten in all — a cheerful flag of red, white, yellow — what a boon.

My hallways are as quiet as I could wish them, but workdays at home are filled with people. Artists and creatives around the country, fundraising online to bring their latest vision to life, seek my professional advice. I love my work, but when it comes to all-or-nothing, time-sensitive crowdfunding, the temperature is high, the intensity contagious.

I take my breaks in the studio down the hall, calming nerve frazzle with steady brush strokes, reducing my world to a single cornflower, a scuff of cloud. Aside from art history I have no training, but this is play, and I have only myself to convince. Free to experiment, I paint for process, for pleasure, without ambition. Canvases large enough to fill my vision and sink into. Landscapes abstracted to the essence of memory, colours bold and unequivocal. Standing at ease, I paint balance for balance.

Ashburton is a town that most people only pass through, but I prefer its 'nothing much' to the show off and shout of cities. It is a place of flat, stark lines, long bridges opening up grand vistas of big sky country. Pea soup sea fog, muddy boots parked at doorways, manure pleasantly stinking up trailers on the street. From the air, the plains are a tidy agricultural palette of green, defined by windbreak avenues. Braided rivers smooth grey ovals of stone from the Alps to the sea, raging in the wet seasons and near dry in summer.

Born and raised in the big city, I am an outsider here. When I talk to the locals I'm too loud, too fast, too much. Mention of a voluntary move from Auckland raises eyebrows. They respond slowly, slightly suspicious. In my first week I encountered a string of mid-Canterbury men, delivering pre-war furniture bought for a song, and my first purchases of new whiteware. They are rugby tall, broad-shouldered, solid, white. I imagine unchanging diets of meat and dairy, beer and scones. The supermarkets are stocked for them: large servings, family packs, barely a single-serve to be found. I start cooking for four, parcelling portions for the freezer.

On weekends I explore, discovering new perspectives from neglected country roads, between rich parcels of earth. I drive the strips that divide the plains, stopping briefly at one-shop destinations: Staveley, Methven, Mayfield. Sometimes, I venture further south to potter in the village hum of Geraldine, and continue inland to the vast, striking expanses of Mackenzie and Tekapo. Returning to the studio, I canvas colour fields of turquoise and vivid lakeside autumn yellow. In mid-winter I stay closer to home, my feet numbing on the chilled concrete floor of a barn the size of a football field, overflowing with cheap, secondhand books. I fill grocery bags with stories until I get hungry, wrapped in layers of merino and a state of bliss.

This is earthquake territory. I have planted myself in the farthest circle of a wide ripple fringing a broken city — relative but tenuous safety. That I have planted myself within reach at all, with the chill of aftershocks still in my bones, is strange. I vow, as I have done before, that this is as far north as I will ever live, but one day I will break this promise again, and suffer for it.

This place is a compromise. Afraid to commit to the south of the south and paint my career into a corner, I have kept a big city within reach, the boundaries wide, loose and unsatisfactory. It is close to where I want to be, but not close enough, and so I live a half-life, one foot out the door. I fall into my old, reclusive refrain: joining official groups of gallery friends and making none, subscribing to art societies that I'll rarely attend, offering service to community groups, only to regret and renege the gift of time. Skimming on the surface, rootless, I play the tired chorus of "should" and "normal" and "settle" until the record skips, I stop pretending, and start planning the next move.

I attach temporarily to the adopted Narnia wardrobe, the generous bay window and playful stained glass, the snug wood panelling. I will look for these again, and hold them close elsewhere. I am playing house, accumulating comfortable, soft-edged, historied possessions. Perhaps I am ready to make this real — to dig deep, claim territory, square off a portion of place for the long term. An elderly antique dealer urges me to buy my own home before I become vulnerable like her; I buy a porcelain teacup and saucer to remind me of her cautionary tale. When the oak leaves turn, an unexpected, life-changing gift — a modest inheritance from the wrench of loss — will make this possible, but in late summer, I can only afford to cast the thought and consider.

I am, many would say, living in the middle of nowhere, but sorrow finds me in this place, as it does everywhere. I am one of the few Arts Foundation employees left standing after a brutal organisational restructure, and the shock and sadness of unjustly losing the trust of those I admired, who have suffered most, reverberate. Familial division too, is distressing; rules of engagement are being renegotiated remotely, following a furious hurling of glass to concrete across the Tasman — my frustration, not for the first time, uncontainable.

My own recycle bin starts to compete with the neighbours. Wine with dinner becomes wine before dinner, after dinner, with lunch. I drink the good stuff from elegant stemware, and so think nothing of it. The rare appearance of friends passing through is at once welcome and strained, as I struggle to cope with the invasion of solitude and silence.

A few blocks away, the swimming lanes are as quiet as the

streets, unlike the feeding frenzy churn of city pools. The new complex is slick, toothbrush clean, natural light bouncing off every surface. A wall of bright yellow tiles greets me with unflagging enthusiasm. This elemental ritual is my daily mass, a foolproof therapy I never question. It is sometimes short, sometimes slow, and sometimes I almost can't be bothered to breathe, but there is no such thing as a bad swim. I find solutions to paintings and more complex problems on the bottom of the pool, glinting like coins in the sunshine.

I hold fast to the smooth calm of conkers collected from the garden — talisman reminders of a London childhood — and as three seasons pass, my canvases fill with joy. Jostling abundant icebergs beneath my bedroom window, flurries of blazing red oak. The calm elegance of camellia by the letterbox, the cheeky spring pop of daffodil and new green. I will take the garden with me when I leave.

HERITAGE

I

You were always up for tackling the state of the world at six in the morning, armed with a milky cup of tea and a thin, brown slice of peanut buttered bread. You listened to my nascent views on current affairs and religion as the portable radio mumbled on the lowboy between our sagging twin beds. As my grandfather snored a symphony down the hall, you fielded my career aspirations from the other side of the room, indulging the blue sky thinking I painted on the low ceiling from the deep pocket of an old feather pillow.

As I navigated the small trials and victories of my primary school years, the holiday routine with you was comforting in its constancy. You instilled in me the delicious habit of second breakfast, carrying our empty cups and chatter to the kitchen, sitting down to shallow bowls of steaming porridge with full cream milk and home-preserved Black Doris plums.

Unlike my maternal grandmother, who bookended the other end of the street and loved to experiment in her kitchen, you weren't interested in cooking, but I delighted in the novelty of your old-fashioned comfort food: beef stew and boiled vegetables, mince on toast with a fried egg on top. Only the awful stench of steak and kidney pie making, which set me gagging and stumbling out to the garden, ever tarnished my winning streak as a no-fuss grandchild.

When we weren't talking our heads off, we were cosied up, side by side in the sitting room, lost in doorstoppers of historical fiction. The tiny cupboard at the end of the hall was an enchanted place, converted to a miniature library that came alive to a naked bulb with a tug of a cord. I gorged on adventure stories from the low shelves — Huckleberry Finn, Tom Sawyer, Treasure Island — until I was tall enough to venture to the locations you armchair travelled.

Your idea of exercise was inspiring — laughing yoga at the local community hall, with a group of intrepid retirees — and a lesson in release that would later serve me well. I cherished our simplest diversions: a drive to the coast in the dear old brown Triumph to gather pinecones for kindling, or learning to play cribbage in the caravan parked in the drive. Evenings together announced themselves with the *Coronation Street* theme and the tap of my grandfather's pipe, when we all settled down for a bit of quiet in the glow of the screen.

In the grown-up years that followed, my visits were less frequent, but we never stopped talking. Phone calls always began with "how are you getting on up there?", regardless of whether I was living north or south, but I was fond of your old habit, and didn't expect you to keep up when I was always on the move.

Into your nineties, you seemed invincible, until the day at the beach when you almost floated out to sea, no longer strong enough to fight the current. Humiliated and heart broken, you declared it your last swim. At least you still have books, I thought, until your reading pace started to slow, your tired eyes struggling, and you feigned lost interest. We continued to talk up a storm, until you became preoccupied with imagined conspiracies in the hall of the rest home and forgot how to use the phone.

In the strangeness of the last room that you would know, your eyes filled with tears when I gently explained that your few treasures would be loved elsewhere. Your three ceramic birds will fly in a blue line on the wall of my brother's home. The stories we shared are on my bookshelf. Your brooches will spruce up my old winter coats. I held your soft, wizened hand, doing my best to provide comfort. You had been wondering, and were so relieved to know what had become of them. It was the only time I ever saw you cry.

I have your thick, coarse hair, your early streak of grey at my temple. I was quick to adopt your quaint and quirky expressions: a "red-letter day" is memorable, "wacko" is great. I like to think that my laugh has the generous warmth of your chuckle. We still talk when I pass the hall table, where your cheerful portrait is propped next to my Nana, as you were on Dublin Street for so many years. I say "Hello Gran" when I reach for your yellow chrysanthemum jug, and smile when I use your Sheffield steel bread knife, still sharp after all these years. When I place apples in your crystal trifle bowl, and serve crumble with your well-worn, silver-plated spoons, I thank you for all that I have inherited, and enabling the gift of a home.

II

It is love at first sight, and I pounce on the real estate agent to request a viewing as soon as the listing appears in early spring. The hero shot dangles a unique heritage property at the entrance to an elevated cul-de-sac, holding out in welcome a light pink camellia in full bloom. The impressive, masculine square of 1930s red brick is topped with an art deco parapet in black, textured stucco and dashing bands of cream. It has been snapped basking languidly in the sun, surrounded by blossoms and lush, hedged garden.

Interior photos reveal a trove of original features: decorative vaulted ceilings, warm wood panelling, and native kauri floorboards. Large, picture frame windows show off scenic views of hilltops and farmland across the valley. The rare bonus of a garage beneath, to spare the car from the ice of Dunedin frosts, ticks the last box on my checklist. It is peaceful, private, and perfect for me.

I obsessively stake out every one of the open homes scheduled, greeting the amused estate agent at the top of the drive each time. Drifting between the rooms, hovering territorially, I gasp and tut-tut when I overhear prospective buyers speak of knocking down the wall between my lounge and office-to-be, or modernising the original kitchen — my favourite room.

I take vengeance on my competitors' philistine notions in a heart-pounding, victorious auction that pushes me to my financial limit. Until the keys are in my hands, I take the short walk from my house-hunting base to my uninhabited new home each morning, lingering outside amidst the glorious birdsong. If it's possible to have a romantic relationship with a house, this is how it begins.

For the first six months in residence, I swing between the elation of this miraculous purchase, and anxiety that something is about to go terribly wrong. I'm one street away from the steepest street in the world, and I catastrophize about landslides. The old trees that provide delicious privacy from the road are perilously close to the power lines, and the sprawling garden, which at this time of year is growing at an astonishing rate, is overwhelming. At night, my skin crawls at the scratching and scuffling of mice in the walls and rats in the roof. I quickly discover that the 80-year-old earthenware pipe to the house is broken, and needs to be dug up and replaced at considerable cost.

I am at once daunted by the responsibility of property ownership, and beyond relieved to be settled. The dread of ever having to leave this place takes root quickly, which surprises me after years of seemingly embracing change. For the first time in my life, it's an emotional wrench to travel, and I feel homesick when staying overnight elsewhere. I have drawn a circle around myself, declaring "I am here", and there is nowhere else I would rather be.

Playing the long game is a challenging transition for a rolling stone-renter used to gathering nothing but steam, but the old house helps me to slow down. The unpleasant task of pulling up the brown, threadbare carpet in the hallway quickly dispels my romantic vision of do-it-yourself, but helps me realise the shift from permanently transient to permanent: this is *my* hall, these are *my* floorboards. It is my nature to notice every minor thing that could be improved, but a tight budget curbs my urges to address everything at once, and I come to learn that envisaged changes don't need to be made today, tomorrow, or maybe ever.

For the first time, I buy a piano. Until now, I have never bought furniture that I couldn't move myself, and invested little, knowing instinctively that it's just a matter of time before I sell up and relocate. The mahogany upright is almost as old as the house, but carefully restored, and I love it fiercely. I haven't played regularly since I was a child, and I start to teach myself all over again without embarrassment, windows opened wide.

On the first of December, I buy a real Christmas tree, and the lounge is transformed with the scent of pine and glow of fairy lights. I host a holiday potluck, and other meals to come, at the old kitchen table spruced in jolly red gingham. Visiting friends and family, who have good-naturedly adapted to the small spaces of my many and various living arrangements over the years, luxuriate in the dedicated guest room, and its soothing dappled light.

On the first day of the new year, still in my pyjamas, I sit down with coffee at the small wooden desk under my bedroom window. Outside, the blackbirds are raiding an ornamental plum tree, hanging low with fruit. On the daisied lawn below, I imagine what will become an English rose garden, a small stone path to an outdoor armchair that catches the afternoon sun. I have never grown roses before, but I'm hopeful that the green thumbs of my maternal grandparents have rubbed off; the recent purchase of a five-year gardening journal is testament to my long-term ambitions. I take in the view across the valley through the steam from my cup: sheep are pottering beneath the poplars, a horse is being put through its morning paces.

Opening a thick, new notebook to the front page, I embark on my first attempt at writing a memoir. Inspired by my newfound appreciation for life on "slow spin", I reflect on my rich and varied years lived at hyperspeed. I acknowledge that navigating life full throttle is "the only way I know how", but I can't unlock what drives my behaviour, and the writing project will founder on my ignorance.

III

Less than three months into the homemaking honeymoon and my desperate embrace of stability, I jump, free fall, from a high cliff of financial security into unplanned unemployment. The second brutal restructure in two years of the national Arts Foundation has set me reeling. This time, the bungled case for change has inadvertently deleted my management role from the budget line without consultation, and in my outrage, I beat the organisation to the punch by resigning. When the implications of the consultant's error finally dawn, Board members are falling over themselves to apologise and retain me, but I'm so appalled by the oversight that I refuse to discuss it.

My resignation is just the latest of many fearless acts of self-assurance that I will find yet another job, but also somewhat irresponsible in the face of mortgage payments and estimates in the thousands for essential plumbing repairs. Typically, it's not the work that has become difficult for me to manage, but communication with the people who employ me. True to form, there is no war chest of savings to soften my fall, and I need to come up with a plan in a hurry. Nevertheless, the stress that this induces is more bearable than what I've been subjected to by my employers, and at least I'm in control.

By the autumn, a flurry of job applications has resulted in a new role as an Analyst at the city's university, and financial calm returns to my home. Crunching operational data is a far cry from the creative juices that flowed through my work in arts crowdfunding, but I welcome the professional rigour that the academic-adjacent position implies. Eventually, my work for the university will evolve into a more strategic, Humanities-oriented role — an ostensible dream job.

As the season turns the valley into an autumnal tapestry, I convert my home office to a dedicated painting studio, and rummage the local secondhand shops for suitable office attire. Now, my workdays begin with a stroll through the Botanic Gardens, where the burbling river guides me to the oldest and most beautiful university in the country.

IV

My sense of belonging in Dunedin is powerful. Its colonial history — so apparent in its abundance of heritage buildings and museums — connects me to my Scottish and English ancestry in a way I haven't felt as strongly elsewhere. My paternal great grandparents arrived in Dunedin by ship, before traversing the rugged width of the South Island to make a life on the West Coast. Dunedin's luxurious stretches of white sand coastline, and dramatic drops from green fields to the sea, revive memories of Cornwall, from where other great grandparents hailed.

At home, I pause my pottering when the faint strains of bagpipe practice in a neighbouring park reach me from across the valley. In the city, I tear up when the kilt-kitted pipe bands fill the air beneath the statue of poet Robert Burns in the annual parade. I'm reminded of my great aunt in the tartan of our clan, her cheeks filling like red balloons with the musical effort that fascinated me as a child.

Dunedin is a UNESCO City of Literature, connecting me with some of the nations greats, and treats its residents to more literary events than I can keep up with. I distract myself from the colder months with plentiful doses of theatre, and enjoy summer evenings watching Shakespeare in the parks.

Historic places are my playground, and here I am spoiled for choice. I roam the fascinating rooms and extensive gardens of Larnach Castle each season, and take in the breath-taking view of Otago Peninsula from the turret. I jump at any excuse to enjoy the splendour of Olveston, and join community tours of other historic homes.

I have called Dunedin home before, but I learn that the relationship is different when you own a plot of land. When I make the steep climb to the top of Flagstaff — the prominent hill that watches over the city — I look down and marvel that this pocket of paradise is mine for the keeping.

My first two years at Cardigan Street is the most stable period of my adult life to date. It is the longest time I have lived in one house since I left the family home at 21. I seem to be thriving, and my new friends and colleagues only know me as positive, energised, and efficient. When, in my third year, at the age of 45, a perfect storm dismantles my relative emotional stability, no one, including me, has foreseen the bonfire my contented life is about to become.

V

On a warm night in January, I am curled up in the large, outdoor armchair nestled in the far corner of my lower garden. I can see the white, lime-chip path in the moonlight, but little else. In the darkness of the witching hour, I catch the light fragrance of 'Tranquillity', a white David Austin rose planted last winter. I have been crying uncontrollably for hours, as quietly as I can, but I suspect it's disturbing the neighbours.

Unable to sleep, my skin crawling with despair, I have moved from the bedroom to the lounge sofa, to here. My mother, who is visiting from Australia, is no doubt struggling to sleep herself, but I have no capacity to attend to her right now. She may very well be frightened of me — I am frightened of myself. The emotional trauma of what has occurred tonight will take us both years to recover from, as much as recovery is possible.

Earlier this evening, I experienced my strangest and most acute breakdown, which she witnessed in high definition, at full volume. Feeling unbearably trapped in my own home by the cumulative tension of a hardworking but volatile mother-daughter relationship, I became, momentarily, inhuman. I was no longer shouting that I was broken, but growling like a beast in a cage, demanding her to get out of my house in a voice that did not sound like my own. It felt like possession, demonic. The horror, shame and guilt that followed has consumed me, and I have been sobbing inconsolably ever since.

The timing and circumstances surrounding my mother's extended visit are unfortunate, to say the least. Soon after her arrival, I start an exciting new professional role, and my determination to impress is generating an increased level of stress. I have, at the same time, fallen in love. For the object of my affection, the timing is all wrong, but I'm high on possibility, and struggling to eat or sleep. I'm difficult to be around, and as long as my brain is in overdrive, and co-habitation impacts my necessary downtime, the emotions I'm experiencing can only intensify.

The country is suffering through a traffic-light phase of prolonged lockdown — the New Zealand government's heavy-handed response to a global pandemic. Effectively been placed under house arrest for months has had its benefits for someone who prefers their own company, but the stringent rules have also limited activities that I have always relied on for balance and well-being: swimming at the local pool, yoga class, visits to the city library, long drives in the country, walking the beach. After a long period of closed borders, my mother has finally been permitted to enter her own country, on the condition that she submits to two weeks of quarantine and stays for at least three months. Leaving Dunedin unexpectedly, when things get rough, is not straightforward.

When dawn breaks, I climb the steps from the rose garden to the house, and make us coffee. I dress and excuse myself, driving to the coast where I sit in the car for hours, staring through the rain out to sea. I still feel like I can't breathe. Underwater with sorrow, I return home and explain to my beloved Mum that I need her visit to end — I need solitude and silence like I need oxygen.

Neither of us can effectively process what has occurred, and this will be the beginning of yet another period of painful estrangement. Those closest to us will only become aware that we have had a very difficult time, which sadly, is par for the course. Only Mum and I knew how extreme my emotions were that night, but after numerous clashes over thirty years, it didn't occur to either of us that it was worthy of psychiatric scrutiny. My explosions of anger had long been associated with inherited paternal traits, and when you have spent much of your adult life behaving abnormally around your parents, it's considered normal behaviour for *you*.

After a few stunned days of sick leave, I return to work prematurely, keeping a low profile, and focusing on basic tasks until I recover from the brain fog that has followed my breakdown. Romantic fantasy-fuelled hypomania soon reclaims its hold, and for the next few months I distract myself with self-imposed overwork as an outlet for my excess energy. Without understanding the need to slow down and emotionally stabilise, my ability to cope with difficult circumstances from this point on will be more limited than ever.

THIS MEANS WAR

Over the course of New Zealand's history, every person who has called it home was either born elsewhere or descended from immigrants. The first to arrive, travelling in canoes from Polynesia, were followed much later by ships of European explorers, and a wave of British colonial settlers. Since the nineteenth century, New Zealand has been home to people from many cultures and walks of life, all granted equal rights under the country's founding document, the Treaty of Waitangi. New Zealand was the first self-governing country in the world to enshrine in law the right for women to vote, and its citizens have long been known for their strong work ethic and easy-going nature.

As a fourth-generation New Zealander, I grew up blind to sex, race, religion, income, and other ways in which humans can be tick-boxed and subjected to prejudice — at least, as blind as I believe it is possible to be. I see people for their common humanity, their ideas and actions, and the distinct blend of personality traits that makes them unique. I was raised to believe that my future is not defined by my demographics, and that I am personally responsible for creating the life to which I aspire.

The cultural backgrounds of my friends, peers, and

romantic partners have always been wide-ranging, and our connections have been enabled by a societal foundation of equality, education, and free speech. For the first four decades of my life, New Zealand was a peaceful place to live, continuing to attract migrants from around the world for the opportunities it affords.

In the year I turned 45, matches that had been lit under these values by those who believe otherwise became a nationwide bush fire. Within three years, the air would become so toxic with identity politics, and race-based rhetoric in particular, that I began to consider leaving the country. At 45, I had been smelling smoke in the public sector for a while, but it wasn't until I naively stepped into the heart of the blaze, as a Strategic Analyst for a university, that I saw the flames.

Between the lines of my job description, my role was expected to enable ideologies to which I am strongly opposed, but it took me time and concerted effort to understand the philosophical conflicts in play, and where I stood in relation to them. I had been slow to realise the extent of the "culture wars", which were not only sweeping New Zealand, but also its closest international allies.

I would come to learn that the ideas I was grappling with, under the umbrella of "social justice", were fuelling a movement to destabilise like-minded nations, and, more broadly, to reframe and undermine the benefits and achievements of Western civilisation. Momentum had been building in academia for years, but it felt to me as if a powerful Little Red Playbook had been planted in every office overnight, and the walls were suddenly reverberating with it.

Until now, my interest in national politics had been limited to election time, and perhaps like many others, I had too easily been seduced by charismatic leadership and persuasive oratory at the expense of values-driven policy. Without looking at the engine under the hood, I had voted for a glamorous leader, lauded internationally for her 'politics of kindness', in the term before the country began to visibly tear itself apart. This was my political awakening.

Initially, seduced by the allure of colourful strategic frameworks, I trusted in good intentions. I put my hand up to benchmark the university against the United Nations Sustainable Development Goals, with a view to inclusive and equitable education, and a healthy and peaceful society. I voluntarily participated in employer-sponsored training in Diversity, Equity and Inclusion (DEI), which challenged my pragmatic belief in focusing limited resources on the needs of the many rather than the few. I willingly contributed an LGBTQ perspective to university workshops aimed at Rainbow Tick accreditation, even though I consider my sexual orientation irrelevant in the workplace.

These initiatives implied that our professional efforts as quasi-civil servants, to equally and efficiently serve all people on our watch, were misguided. Within the university and in the media, senior academics were radically reframing New Zealand's majority population, and education's underpinning concept of merit, as white supremacy. The work of university staff became increasingly focused on moving the goal posts of employee recruitment, and student entrance and achievement, based on ethnicity.

The red carpet was being rolled out for a small percentage of the population that identified as Māori, and our continued employment and promotion became dependent on unquestioning compliance with this approach. For the first time in my life, I was working alongside colleagues with insufficient credentials, explicitly recruited based on ancestry, and consequently emboldened to claim ethnic superiority. Even the most restrained and respectful opposition to race-based policy resulted in staff and students declaring they did not feel "safe", and university endorsement of different working arrangements to "protect" them from challenging views.

As the university embarked on a major rebrand, in an effort to distance itself from its colonial founders, it was no longer considered appropriate to voice pride in my British ancestry. Many of those who had helped to build a globally connected, first-world nation were being disparaged and reduced to "old white men". In personal and professional arenas, I was expected to acknowledge the "privilege" of being white-skinned, with middle-class parents — undermining their successful efforts to create a better life from humble beginnings.

I instinctively balked at what seemed to me unfairness, but my integrity as a professional, and a citizen, demanded that I dig deeper to unpack and understand. I began to read widely and deeply, in a spirit of robust internal debate. I refreshed my knowledge of national history, paid attention to Māori leaders, and spent hours reflecting on the Treaty of Waitangi and its contemporary interpretations. I tuned in more acutely to higher education trends and current affairs, and sought out insightful commentary on critical race theory, gender, and cancel culture.

While my colleagues were choosing wholesale adoption of social justice with revolutionary zeal, or stewing in fearful silence, my mind became preoccupied with arguments for equal rights and meritocracy versus affirmative action with a view to equity. I wrangled democracy versus co-governance with a view to decolonisation. I considered the implications for me personally, the institution for which I worked, and tertiary education generally. I considered the implications for the peace and prosperity of New Zealand. Determined to be a "good human", I wrestled with values I had largely taken for granted for four decades, and searched my soul on all fronts.

At first glance, the concept of social justice appeared admirable, but on closer examination, I began to understand its complexities and limitations. I had observed over the years that New Zealanders generally are politically apathetic, perhaps as a result of regular elections, which had until now kept the country relatively close to the centre of the spectrum since the Second World War. I was brought up in an environment that did not encourage politics as a topic of conversation, which was not unusual among my peers, but I considered my general knowledge of social history sound. It seemed unlikely that many around me, who outwardly supported social justice and its enabler identity politics, had attempted to connect the dots between the ideas to which they virtue-signalled, and the kind of future these ideas might manifest.

Over the course of the year, and those that followed, I observed that, far from the societal harmony and boosted productivity envisaged by exponents, identity politics and DEI policies were predominantly cultivating and giving voice to intolerance, disrespect, and entitlement. I was not alone in my concern that social justice initiatives were consuming considerable tax-payer resources, and distracting people from the primary purpose of their education and employment, but a university was no place to question what had come to feel like the religion of woke.

My contribution to the government's landslide victory was a devastating reckoning, as I watched the country reap what it had sown. Inside and outside the walls of the university, the frequency of organised protest, racism from Māori, sexism from women, and anti-heterosexual rhetoric was unprecedented. The hostility I was witnessing shocked me to the core, and dismayed friends who had migrated to New Zealand from homelands ravaged by apartheid, and countries with oppressive regimes.

Rational debate was being strangled, and hysteria and hyperbole reigned; opposing views were quickly reframed as "hate speech" and "violence", and their impact as "fear" and "trauma". Opponents of race-based policies were loudly and publicly labelled racists intent on "genocide", and "traitors" of the same race were no exception. The English language is always changing, but the speed at which definitions were evolving was suddenly mind-bending. Instead of helping to bridge the gaps between us, language became the shifting sands on which we took one step forward and two steps back from one other; the politically correct word to use six months ago might be perceived as a slur today.

Around the university and across the country, a wave of Māori language, understood by a thimble of the population, was suddenly disorienting and disarming the English-speaking masses. Mainstream communication channels were obstructed by the static of bilingual peppering, while the country and government ministries were renamed by stealth. Navigation on foot, by car, and online was slowed by the noise of signage overrun with two languages, with the least understood given priority. In the midst of a pandemic, the plague of public health posters became increasingly incomprehensible to the majority. Speaking Māori and demonstrating "cultural competency" became explicitly linked to employment around the country, and it pained me, as a lover of language and culture, to be simultaneously force-fed and gagged.

Full immersion in the culture wars, and my role in inadvertently fuelling the belly of the beast, brought my mental health to its knees. I had been tasked with collaboratively updating the university's vision, mission, and strategic objectives —initially considered an honour and career highlight. As I realised my staunch opposition to the fundamental changes afoot, something inside me broke. Universities, which had been places of enlightenment, had become engulfed in darkness. My personal and professional relationships were under strain, and I had never seen my country so divided. My sense of belonging — in a university, in the public sector, and in New Zealand — was dissolving, and my grief was overwhelming.

It was another two years before the next election, when New Zealanders would have an opportunity to politically course correct, but there was no guarantee that they would do so in sufficient numbers, or that a change of government would be enough to turn the tide. Realising that my reaffirmed values of equality, respect, personal responsibility, and free speech could not harmoniously co-exist with the dominant narrative that had swamped every sector in which I enthusiastically engaged, I spiralled into a state of despair.

THE BABY AND THE BATHWATER

Despite the unsettling spring gusts and snowy blasts, a September garden in Dunedin is a sight for sore eyes after months of dormancy and darkness. Each stroll around the house offers up new delights. Outside the front door, a watercolour primrose in drizzled lilac gathers its double petticoats, and nudges me to check on the recent settlement of miniature cyclamens nearby; their angelic feathers, fluttering beneath a trellis of jasmine, confirm all is well. On the slope opposite, foxgloves are shooting high, surrounded by delicate white bells of onion weed and awakening fuchsia.

At the top of the path, a terracotta pot of blue and yellow striped pansies distracts from a cluster of tired snowdrops that have put up their feet until next year. From the high mound of the letter box, I pause to watch the exquisitely crafted earrings of a kowhai tree dancing against the blue sky. Its royal yellow carpet invites me down the drive, where a new hydrangea is doing well, awaiting the companionship of lobelia and snapdragon, germinating in the garden shed.

Turning onto the old bricked terrace, new poppies are streaking up, giant and boisterous, already too large for their pot. The first bold sweet pea shoots are introducing themselves in the rockery, and a cotillion of daffodils in lemon and cream welcome them to the party. Looking down on the lower lawn, rose bushes are growing fast and strong, as paper daisy seedlings, inspired by their energy, peek out from a giant grey pot, blinking in the sunshine. Around the corner, heading back to the house, a proliferation of pastel granny's bonnets gossip beside the clothesline.

The satisfying, soil-dusted efforts of my three years here are all around me, but there is always more to do. There is much transplanting at this time of year, ensuring that each self-seeded plant has its best chance to thrive, and doesn't crowd its neighbour. An overabundance of cornflower seedlings should be relocated from the rockery, and the California lilac needs more room. I scribble with a pencil as I hover, bow, and inspect, listing weekend tasks and gardening centre purchases: potting mix, spray for the roses. In September, I can't imagine ever leaving this place. I have no idea that it will be my last spring as custodian of this garden.

Just as winter seems to be over, temperatures plummet in the first half of October. I regret planting the sweet peas so early, as wind, rain and hail batters the garden. From my office in the university's nineteenth-century Gothic clock tower, I watch snow blanket the lawn and white out the windowpanes, muting the campus as people stay indoors, cosied up to the old cast iron radiators.

Today, the snow is a welcome distraction from the internal reverberations of the weekend. On Friday, mainstream media picked up on an article in a national journal, published by a prominent professor, lambasting the university for what he perceives as white supremacy, privilege and meritocracy. It is just the latest example of many, to internally undermine educational institutions in the name of social justice, but it is the one that tips my balance.

After months of navigating a recent injection of government-sponsored racial tension in the workplace, and the realisation that my role is being oriented to stoke more of the same, reading this article is the tripwire for the bipolar episode that ultimately leads to diagnosis. The article's allegations, which I consider inflammatory, fallacious, and doom-laden, trigger such overwhelming grief for my career and my country that it derails me overnight. As I watch the snow flurries repaint my surroundings, I am staring into a chasm of depression so deep that my brain rears back and revolts to hypomania. I'm convinced that my only option is to change everything about my circumstances as quickly as possible.

Within days, I resign from a position for which — politics aside — I am ideally suited. I set myself up as an independent contractor, and start interviewing with prospective clients. If only I had stopped there, I might have changed my circumstances for the better, but typically I am compelled to overcorrect, and throw the baby out with the bathwater. Convincing myself of more professional opportunities, I exchange the place I love for a larger city where I have vowed to never live again. Dismissing the cautious option of renting, I elect to sell my forever home and buy elsewhere.

Internally, I am in a state of knee-jerk panic, but on the outside I have switched to marketing mode. I sell the plan for my latest personal rebrand to those around me as if it's the best idea in the world. My family is surprised, but friends and colleagues call me brave and inspiring. No one recognises what it is really going on, except that I'm acting typically for me.

I am vaguely aware that something about this particular over-the-top response feels different, but I have nothing in place to help slow me down and examine it. For the first time, my brain is functioning at such high speed that I can hardly keep up with myself. I am thinking and acting so fast that I'm not emotionally processing, and by the time it comes to pack up my beloved home, I'm numb.

By the end of October, the garden is growing at rapid pace with warmer weather, but I am no longer paying attention. The budding climbing rose on the slope is invisible to my preoccupied gaze, and purple viola, sprawling happily near the top of the path, receive half-hearted acknowledgement. The flowering japonica and shooting white iris by the clothesline go unnoticed, and the top-heavy sunflowers are left unstaked.

FAKE GRASS

I had been propelled to clean sweep my circumstances, and so they were. When, after an intensive campaign of change, every task on my list had been completed, it was as if a spell lifted. Seemingly becalmed for the first time in four months, I looked around me and no longer recognised my life. In that moment, a powerful depressive wave was hovering above me, tipped to crash with such force that I would struggle to keep my head above water for the next six months.

I had exchanged a beloved heritage home, in a peaceful Dunedin valley, for a new cookie-cutter townhouse in the heart of a city that I associated with earthquake trauma. I had replaced a modest, manageable home loan with an extravagant and daunting one. Upset by reminders of my Dunedin home, I had immediately sold or donated many of the treasured possessions I had brought with me, purchasing instead modern furniture with no history. I had traded my semi-rural outlook for a view of a doctor's car park, and the waste incinerator of a large hospital.

Beyond my gate, the lush hills and quiet hum of a small city had been swapped for the concrete sprawl, grinding traffic, and ongoing rebuild of a large one. The business of my first contracting client in the private sector could not be further removed from the creative and intellectual spaces in which I thrived. Not for the first time, I had moved to a place where I had no family or friends, and would largely ride the fall out of hypomania alone.

Four months ago, on a spontaneous and desperate reconnaissance mission to Christchurch, I had seen only what I wanted to see. My bullet train impulses — laser focused on the logistics of transition and future state — had impatiently dismissed any thoughts that would be an obstacle to progress. Radical change at frantic pace could not permit serious consideration of the damage that the wrong environment could do to my well-being, the pressure of a massive financial commitment on fledgling self-employment, or the violence to my psyche that would come from abandoning the place, home, and work I loved. Suspending disbelief had been essential for writing a new story that otherwise made no sense.

Having unpacked every box, and put the house in perfect, show home order within three days of arrival, I sat down on a minimalist slab of grey sofa and stared through the glass of a sliding door. A passionate gardener, who celebrated the first rose of the season, and spoke to plants as if they were friends, I was now the owner of a tiny square of fake grass in a bare concrete courtyard. I must have been out of my mind.

If the deep, contented roots I had put down over the past three years in Dunedin weren't strong enough to stop me from impulsive transplantation, surely this cycle was never going to end. For the first time in my life, I felt out of control and afraid of myself, and it was in that moment that I sensed I was dealing with something other than "just me". For the first time, I knew that I needed professional help. Until I figured out what that looked like, it was sink or swim. Thankfully, I'm a strong swimmer.

As depression pushed me under, my cognitive functioning began to falter. My brain, so recently high performing, was now unreliable as it began to buffer and freeze. Normally a quick and voracious reader, the ability to digest paragraphs of text was eluding me, as an invisible drill powered into the right side of my skull. An eagle-eyed, trained proofreader, I was now skipping words as I wrote, and hesitating over homonyms, my brain stalling at now/know, their/there. My elegant cursive became a stuttering scrawl. In emotional discussions on the phone with family, I struggled to summon and sound words.

A usually enthusiastic cook, I lost interest in food that had become tasteless. Preparing a cup of tea in the kitchen became a Herculean effort of coordination, and playing my piano was out of the question. I paused blankly in doorways, having forgotten the reason for entering a room. Driving in a city I knew well, I was occasionally seized with disoriented panic, imagining I was lost, or confusing the actions associated with traffic lights.

Analysing my finances in a spreadsheet, which I had recently handled with ease, was suddenly beyond me. The anxiety of no longer being equipped to manage my life became overwhelming, and every effort was made more difficult by crushing fatigue. I was going to bed before it was dark, and on waking felt as if I hadn't slept at all. The effects of depression were more severe than any I had experienced before.

My brain had crashed two weeks after starting work with my first client, and shortly after, yet another pandemic lockdown required staff to work from home. In my case, this was a merciful gift, as I could now work without the distractions of a busy, open-plan office, and cope and crumple in private. I could gently talk myself through tasks aloud, like a nurse to a patient, as my concentration wobbled in the sliver of space between two computer screens.

With my working memory shot, I started scribbling detailed lists of everything that I had to do. The project for which I was contracted involved diverse tasks that required only short bursts of concentration, and as long as I was talking shop and not required to emotionally engage, I could effectively converse online. It seemed miraculous, when I was mentally on my knees, but the client was impressed with my work.

When you're trying to pull off a high wire act, you need to keep looking forward: look down, and you're doomed. I desperately wanted to stop completely and rest, but I couldn't afford it. Driven by financial survival, and the fear of losing my professional credibility along with everything else, I rallied my faculties when I was on the clock, only to collapse with a headache and exhaustion at the end of every day. It wasn't sustainable, but I was taking life one hour at a time.

I relied on coping mechanisms that I didn't identify as coping mechanisms, as I always had. My upbringing had embedded the importance of exercise, nutrition, and self-discipline. Launching my terrified ten-year-old self onto a lake, my mother had taught me to sail, and breathe under a boat that had capsized. In my early teens, I had run alongside my father in preparation for competing cross-country, and pulled myself out of the mid-winter mud as he cheered me from the sideline. As an adult, being able to separate mood from healthy habits, and attempt what seemed impossible, had helped to keep me afloat.

Now, even with my sense of identity almost completely unravelled, my deeply entrenched, military-style routine insisted I eat, exercise, and maintain some semblance of order, whether I felt like it or not. I got up when my alarm went off in the morning and made the bed. I sat down to work at the same time each day, and paid the bills. I kept the fruit bowl filled and the house tidy. I stuck to my swimming schedule, and forced myself out to the coast for long walks on the beach.

With the limited mental capacity I had outside of work hours, I embarked on a mission to understand what was going on with me. I needed help, but I didn't know how to even begin articulating what I was experiencing. It didn't occur to me to just show up at a doctor's clinic in a state of total confusion. The self-imposed upheaval I had just been through was extreme, but it wasn't new. I was a trained researcher and analyst by trade, so I started compiling data.

I created a timeline of the last 30 years, starting at the age of 16 when my father left, prompting the painful move from the 1940s seaside cottage that my family had long called home. I filled columns with age, year, location, residence, professional roles, relationships, and key life events. I had to dig deep to remember. Until now, I had instinctively avoided looking back, which made me feel dizzy and disoriented. Now, I stared unflinchingly into my past, and the patterns that emerged were staggering.

Since leaving my mother's home at the age of 21, I had, on average, relocated every year, often to another city or country. The home in which I had lived the longest, and been most happy, was the home I had just abandoned. Since first graduating university, I had held 22 jobs for an average of one year each. Most roles were aligned to my interests and qualifications, and several I had considered dream jobs. Every resignation and relocation over the past 30 years had been my decision.

As I logged these annual upheavals, and recalled the times I had washed up at my parents' doors from the latest shipwreck, it occurred to me that my adult life had been a case of chronic financial instability. I knew the weight of credit card debt all too well. I had often borrowed money from parents, and once, a partner and a grandparent. These loans were almost always repaid, but it was not uncommon for me to be in debt.

I was not often lonely, but often alone. Of seven serious relationships, three had involved living under the same roof. Engaged three times, I had married and divorced once. I had mostly considered myself happily single, but now I acknowledged that it had long felt like I was incapable of sustaining a relationship. A major depressive episode at the age of 22 was clearly linked to the struggle to clarify my sexual orientation, and come out to my family.

I could recall seven episodes of depression that impaired brain functioning and impacted on my ability to work full-time. I noted over twenty less severe episodes, occurring once a year on average. There was nothing random about these episodes — I could clearly pinpoint the trigger — but it would take me longer to understand the relationship between emotion, communication, hypomania and depression, which had been underlying the strange combination of success and self-sabotage.

Without any preconceived idea of what I am looking for, or the psychiatric terminology that would later become familiar, I begin throwing words into an online search engine in an effort to name the patterns in my life. The results quickly paint a picture of a connection between extraordinary confidence and productivity, destabilising emotion, and debilitating depression. The rollercoaster I have been on for the last 30 years is consistent with the criteria for Bipolar Disorder Type II.

THAT EXPLAINS A LOT

THE GP

I'm trying to focus on the notebook sitting open in my lap, and my blurry bullet points for discussion. My eyes are teary, my glasses are steaming up. I've only just sat down in the GP's consulting room, but I'm soon overwhelmed. The doctor gently invites me to remove the mandatory pandemic mask, and take a tissue from the box in her outstretched hand. Frustrated, I take a moment to pull myself together; what I have to say is too important not to articulate clearly.

I've lost count of the general practitioners that have added pages to my unexceptional medical file over the course of my gypsy life. This one appears close to my age of 46, and a little tired, as general practitioners often are, but patient. Her face is almost completely hidden by a disconcerting mask that makes me think of chemical warfare, but her eyes and voice are kind. I have only recently moved to the city, so we have never met before, but I trust her.

When I've done my best to regroup, I give her the lay of the land as I see it, based on two weeks of self-analysis and desktop research. She listens attentively as I summarise, for the first time, 30 years of destabilising emotional highs and lows. I explain that the spontaneous relocation I've just completed is the latest in a string of extreme responses to difficult circumstances. I share my deep sadness at having abandoned a place I love. In response to her questions, I tell her that I live alone, and have no family or friends in the city.

As a slim rectangle of sun begins to warm the corner in which I sit, she encourages me to keep talking. Feeling mercifully unhurried, I describe the nature of the depression that is currently impairing my cognitive functions. While I'm not capable of anything more than keeping my head above water right now, I'm fearful of inevitably returning to a state of mind that I suspect is hypomania. I no longer trust in my perception of reality, or my ability to make sound life decisions. Frankly, I'm afraid of myself, and what I'm capable of without intervention. I share my hypothesis that I'm in Bipolar Type II territory, and ask how I can arrange for a specialist evaluation.

Following a series of questions to indicatively eliminate other possibilities, the GP agrees with my line of thinking, and outlines a plan for further investigation and immediate support. She strongly encourages me to reduce my working hours in order to rest, and hears out my fearful protests about being newly self-employed. She explains that she serves her own well-being by working only part-time, and this gives me the courage to do the same. Over the next few weeks, the knowledge, advice, and empathy of my GP, will help to guide my lifeboat around the rocks and onto the sand.

THE NATUROPATH

A naturopath is usually my first port of call before a GP, but under the circumstances I have covered my bases, and scheduled appointments with both. With a track record of relocating every year on average, I have benefitted from many natural health practitioners, but access to this particular one at this particular time is a gift for which I will always be grateful. The long drive between us decides that today we meet in a virtual square, but the welcome force of her vibrant smile, framed by a chic black bob, instantly dissolves the screen. Having met before, we quickly adapt to our online room and get down to business, like two enthusiastic geeks in a study group.

I discover that she is not only a naturopath and nutritionist, but also a registered mental health nurse. Leveraging her experience as an integrative practitioner, she efficiently considers my recent breakdown, and analyses my list of physiological complaints: headaches, body aches, fatigue, atypically short hormonal cycles, brain fog. In a subsequent session, we will focus on the management of perimenopause, but today she gives me the homework of blood tests, as she explains the role of specific vitamins, minerals and fats for supporting mental health. She suggests herbs with calming properties, from which I can make tea: valerian root, chamomile, passionflower, lavender.

Together, we outline a plan to serve my recovery and complement psychiatric and psychological support. We discuss holistic methods for managing stress: exercise, yoga, meditation. When I describe my current difficulty with reading, she suggests video resources in lieu of books. Like my GP, she is aware of new research on the role of nutrition for managing depression, and points me in the direction to learn more.

THE RESEARCHER

The city to which I have recently returned in a hypomanic haze is where I started my postgraduate journey in the humanities ten years ago. Across the University of Canterbury campus, exploring very different territory, was a Professor of Clinical Psychology, interested in the role of nutrition for the treatment and prevention of depression, anxiety, and stress. In the same year that I am seeking psychiatric help, her book on nutrients for mental resilience is hot off the press, and her free course is being taken up by health practitioners around the country and beyond.

As I wait out the two months between my first visit to the GP and my psychiatric evaluation, I learn as much about nutrients for brain health as my currently struggling brain allows. Starting with the findings of her research, I start exploring the possibility of an alternative to the medication typically prescribed by psychiatrists for managing bipolar. I am keen to avoid a host of documented side effects, and preserve the treasured creativity that orthodox medication is infamous for suppressing.

THE COUNSELLOR

My counsellor steps back for a moment from the busy, hieroglyphed whiteboard, black marker in hand. We are so deeply engaged in energised discussion, and I'm so in my element, that I'm on the edge of my seat. Anyone walking into the room could be mistaken for thinking this is a workshop for a business start-up. My allocated time with her, for my first session of brief intervention talking therapy, was officially up over an hour ago.

The professional titles held by the brilliant, middle-aged woman standing in front of me, in comfortable clothes and necklaced with an artistic silver cross, are mental health clinician and registered nurse. She is also an opera singer, a pianist, and a powerful combination of straight talk and motherly warmth. I am, thankfully, eligible for the stopgap service of five publicly-funded sessions with her, but this first meeting alone is one of the most empowering gifts I ever receive.

She is, understandably, finding it remarkable that outside this room I am struggling to mentally function, dragging myself through the day one hour at a time. I had arrived at the clinic fully prepared to work, like the professional consultant that I am, despite being hobbled by depression and on the verge of tears. Given sufficiently powerful motivation, I have always been able to rally in short bursts, and in this case, my thirst for insight into my past is fierce.

Armed with my recently crafted timeline, and summary of the high drama experienced over three decades, I had sat down beside her desk and concisely outlined the situation in which I now find myself. I explained that I want to "reverse relocate" back to Dunedin, but I can't start this process until I emotionally stabilise. Based on the effects of a depression more debilitating than I've experienced before, this could take several months; in the meantime, I welcome her support.

My timeline highlights a clear pattern of physical flight from difficult circumstances, but it doesn't explain the pattern of thinking that prompts it. Together, our analytical minds efficiently examine my values, and consider swathes of emotional territory that other mental health practitioners might have taken weeks to attempt. In the process, we land on two unfamiliar concepts that instantly pour light into the jumbled room of my painful past: Maslow's hierarchy of needs, and distress tolerance.

It is in this counsellor's room that I begin to understand why I am relentlessly motivated, when things "aren't working", to demolish and relay my foundations in pursuit of greater heights. Considering my pattern of flight through the prism of Maslow's pyramid framework, it becomes clear that I have always been prepared to abandon employment, property, and relationships that I believe are not serving my self-esteem, strength, freedom, and potential.

Introducing me to the concept of distress tolerance, the counsellor suggests different methods of "sitting with" uncomfortable emotions to process them, instead of running a mile. This is more easily said than done, but I'm open to trying; a backlog of negative emotions affects me physically in a way that soon becomes unbearable, generating internal pressure that manifests as migraines and nausea. There's more going on here, and I need to dig deeper. I need to examine my triggers and default responses, to understand how I become so overwhelmed and desperate in the first place.

THE PSYCHIATRIST

The well-groomed, elderly Dutchman, sitting opposite in sky-blue shirt and tie, has the soulful eyes and gentle manner of a mystic. Like my naturopath, the psychiatrist I have sought out for his specialist expertise lives many miles from me, but the strength of his life force is not diminished by the screen that connects us. I am immediately comfortable in his presence, and prepared for someone who might be considered a little unorthodox. Amongst the generic information required of a registered medical professional, his online profile glitters with words that intrigue and draw me to him: he is interested in instinct and intuition, soul and spirit, arts and culture, anthroposophy.

The purpose of our eye-wateringly expensive, 90-minute session is a full psychiatric assessment. I have been informed that completing the process may require more than one session, but otherwise I'm unsure of what to expect. It quickly transpires that we must step through a clearly structured format, which will resurface as bold headings in a clinical report: demographics, presenting issues, psychiatric and medical history, family history, personal and developmental history, current mental state, and finally, diagnosis and treatment plan. As the psychiatrist keeps up a steady stream of note-taking, I dedicate my efforts to concision and clarity as I summarise decades of my life, enduring gut-wrenching memories at each turn. For the past three days, I have been completely beside myself and drowning in fear, but today I am determined to keep it together.

Just over an hour after I introduce myself as "out of control and needing my head examined", I am granted an unequivocal outcome that confirms my recent hypothesis: I am suffering from a textbook case of Bipolar Disorder Type II. While this efficiently delivered information comes as a massive relief, empowering me to name and manage symptoms that until now have managed me, the diagnosis is associated with a hopeless, widely accepted limitation: chronic, incurable mental illness.

As we discuss my response to diagnosis, and options for treatment, his eyes are kind, his mood buoyant. He nods and smiles in validation when I share that my long-held sense of being different from those around me, like a comic book hero with unusual strengths and weaknesses, wasn't a figment of my imagination. He assures me that, based on everything I do to support my well-being, I have an excellent prognosis. He encourages me to think of bipolar not as an illness or disorder, but as a gift to harness and a demon to tame.

While he recommends a commonly prescribed pharmaceutical mood stabiliser, he is supportive of my interest in first exploring a nutrient-based approach under the guidance of my naturopath. Over the course of the year, with professional monitoring and a generous dose of patience with experimentation, my brain health is boosted with a tailored combination of quality nutritional supplements. We land on a simplified combination to support my ongoing management of Bipolar Type II that is free of side effects, and one game-changing nutrient in particular that provides me with effective, non-addictive, on-demand relief from the physiological impacts of stress: magnesium.

As the virtual clock ticks closer to the end of our session, the psychiatrist points me towards a host of resources provided by the mental health institute from which he hails. He encourages me to systematically monitor my mood and health indicators daily, as a method of identifying periods when I need more rest and support, and preventing challenging circumstances escalating into full-blown bipolar episodes.

Having learned of my love of reading, he suggests the works of Dr Kay Redfield Jamison, launching a bookshelf of bipolar memoirs from which I will draw strength over the next two years. As we speak of my passion for the arts, which he explains is common among people who suffer with bipolar, he encourages me to "name and demarcate" my illness through writing, painting, and other creative outlets.

Over the next few weeks, as sharing my diagnosis and what it means "connects the dots" and "explains a lot" for friends, family, and former colleagues, I begin the long process of orienting myself to this new reality. I believe that diagnosis has demystified my eventful life to date, which I come to think of as Life Before, but I'm yet to grasp what it means for my future — Life After.

All that I am certain of is that books are central to my life, and fulfilling my dream of being a writer has been disrupted and delayed for too long. I will never request a pharmaceutical prescription to manage bipolar, and we will never meet again, but four weeks after my session with the mystic psychiatrist, as I sit surrounded by the rich autumn colours of my newly planted courtyard garden, I start to envisage the shape of this book.

For many years, a recurring dream saw me driving off the road in an uncontrollable vehicle. Often, I was trying to drive from the backseat, where I couldn't see the road or reach the gears. Sometime in my distant past I had interpreted this dream as premonition, and attached a fear of suicide or death by car accident, which explains why I'm such a cautious driver in real life. Shortly after diagnosis, the dream changes: I do drive off the road over a cliff, but my car can fly. The emotional release is incredible: I've got this. I'm going to be ok.

ACCLIMATIZE

ALL THAT MATTERS

I was a poet first. Perhaps I will always be a poet first — an extractor, a distiller, a perfumer — in search of beauty and power. A poem champions concision and precious time, cutting through the noise to the bloody heart of experience with pure voice. The form is forgiving of interrupted routine, life upheaval, distortion. It is possible to write a poem in the dark, crouching down to spy the world through a keyhole.

Spoken word — when fear of public speaking is overcome with gentle force and practice — is poetry meets music making. I am conductor channelling cadence, a weaver of the arts. The best poetry strips a performer bare, sometimes with the first words, sometimes the last. There are poets who strip boldly, pants first, and others unexpectedly, at the last moment, with the twist of a single button. I tend to strip slowly, line by line, layer by layer, holding eye contact, pausing for you to appreciate, daring you to look away.

There are poems that halt the spin of the world, like a finger pressed to the globe, just for a moment. The stillness is a gift: I can sit with it, take a good hard look, consider. Other poems carry me away on their own particular stream, and there is liberation in surrendering to someone else's flow, when you can trust in the craft. My own poems serve memory, snapshots of former self surprising me as I pack and unpack, moving through time, from place to place.

I am not a scrawler, a stream of consciousness writer. Watch me in a room with others tasked with storytelling: I will draft a sentence in the time others fill a page. I appear almost motionless, but my mind is racing: strategising, establishing purpose, analysing, filtering tactics. I am choosing each word like an expensive gift, a weapon, assessing its weight, the feel of it in my hands, its suitability for the task. A wrong word will make for a different trajectory, a different outcome, unintended consequences. A wrong word will change the shape of the world I am building, like a foundational brick misaligned. For decades, I interpreted this glacial pace, this seemingly atypical exceptional care, as evidence of my limitations as a writer. I underestimated the value of being a poet first, and an architect always.

Page purging is associated with mental detoxing, emergency therapy, not the kind of writing to be read. My journals are dull, relentlessly repetitive, echoing with the sounds you might hear from someone broken at the bottom of a well. Open one at any page, and you will encounter the same words on a tormenting loop: stress, struggle, endure, hopeless, despair. For me, journalling is exorcism not art, a desperate process of expelling the negatives — can't, don't, resent, hate — and searching desperately for a way out.

My notebooks have always been essential, but when I am gone, my executor will find only one. Looking back upends me, and so my notebooks are destroyed when they have fulfilled their purpose — unceremoniously torn into ragged squares and recycled along with empty cans and cardboard packaging.

The journals that have stood the test of time and line my shelves are filled with the words of others. For years, I marvelled at their ability to dash off a day, capture a mood or a moment in coherent soundbites instead of a ramble or rant; I was slow to appreciate the crucial role of editor. Perhaps, if sufficiently abridged, my notebooks could inform, inspire and provide solace as others do, but I prefer to leave art behind.

I am watched over — as woman, as writer — by a triumvirate of patron saints, channelled with a whispered incantation: Katherine, Virginia, Vita. Soul, mind, and body, I am all of them, at once: the Antipodean torn by place, the haunted word spinner with ink-stained fingers, the English snob in gumboots with an eye for the softer sex. Their three-way rivalry is alive and well, fuelling me to write more with less, to be more, need less, desire always. Together, they watch me from the shelves, wrap around me on the walls, envying, perhaps, the precious time and liberation to shout life and love from the rooftops.

They have been with me since the beginning, their names the stuff of reading lists: Mansfield, Woolf, Sackville-West. Their patience with me is astonishing; I would forgive them for thinking that it might never happen, that I would never sit still long enough, often enough, to finish anything of note. There is no slower germination than an aspiring writer relying on inspiration or the right mood to start, continue, complete. For years, I was so spellbound by art and artists that I mistook dedication for magic. Routine, which for years I consistently applied to everything *but* writing, is the trick I missed but caught on to just in time. It is the daily practice, the fierce protection of hours, the turning up, the steady process of working through, that writes a book.

When you meet me for the first time and ask what I do, I will call myself a writer — this is what my life is about now. At first, I wrote poems sometimes. Now, I write because it is all that matters — the necessity to create has been tested and proved, and the surge of stories is unabating. Finally, I found the words to splint my breaks and ladder me out of the well: hypomania, depression, cognitive distortion. Soon, other words will stand me upright and propel me forward: honesty, integrity, confidence. Each day, I write myself into the driver's seat, steering towards the light, to reconcile, reclaim, and honour my reasons to be.

TYPICAL

In the far north of Thailand, at the entrance to a small, sumptuous temple of red and gold, is an old wooden ceiling painted aquamarine and cobalt blue. I am standing beneath, aged 24, tilting my head back to take in the decorative story above. Eight figures in orange robes sit Buddha-style, with the white squares of an astrological calendar. Around them, creatures of the earth crouch and coil, prowl and prance, soar against the fields of blue. The painting appears humble compared to the opulence of the hall that lies beyond, but when my memories of this temple and its like have faded twenty years later, the photo I take of this ceiling will still arrest my steps, and hold me captive from its wooden frame on the wall.

An astrological chart was commissioned by my mother soon after I was born, but I didn't see it until many years later, when it was uncovered during a house move. Like an archival treasure, it required careful handling, its pages browned and ragged, the hard folds threatening to split each page in four. Ballpoint blue handwriting captured the exact place and time of my birth, the position of the planets, my relationship to fire, earth, air and water. The faded black ink of a typewriter outlined my positive and negative traits, and specific aspects of my personality. At the age of seventeen, my character was well established, and the accuracy of the chart, written before I could even speak, was astonishing.

I am a typical Aries — a colourful astrological sign infamous for its confidence and caprice. Show me any list of Aries descriptors, and every one will apply. I am, and have always been by default, passionate, enthusiastic, talkative and courageous. I am also impulsive, impatient and pugnacious. Aries traits have both fuelled my rash endeavours, and enabled me to find a new way forward when I derail; I am versatile, adaptable, and generally optimistic. I am brave, energetic, and entrepreneurial.

Curiously, Aries traits are so closely aligned to the diagnostic criteria for hypomania, that they would help to explain away symptoms of mental illness for thirty years. When it came to digesting my belated diagnosis, it took concerted effort to understand the nature of Bipolar Type II, in order to recognise where my exuberant personality stops and abnormality begins. Later, for the same reason, it will take time for people to trust in my recovery.

Bipolar plays out differently for people, depending on individual circumstances, and some may grapple with one end of the pole more often than the other. Historically, hypomania had been more frequent and destabilising for me than depression. Diagnostic criteria for hypomania encompass elevated mood or irritability, in addition to three or four of the following: abnormally high self-esteem, decreased need for sleep, more talkative or pressure to keep talking, racing thoughts or more ideas than usual, distractibility, increase in goal-directed behaviour, and pleasurable activities with high likelihood of negative consequences. The fine distinction then, between my "classic Aries" personality and hypomanic symptoms, is the extent to which my behaviour diverges not only from what might be considered normal by others, but what is normal for *me*. Imagine then, a full-blown Aries in the grips of hypomania. Quite a handful.

In order to identify the early warning signs of a hypomanic episode, and self-impose protective restraint, I need to pay attention to the *extremities* of my thinking, the *scale and pace* of my supposed solutions, and the *level of risk* I am entertaining. It's easy to be seduced by the euphoria of hypomania, but much harder to deal with the consequences of my actions. If I don't catch and wrangle the early warning signs, I may rebound from hypomania into a depressive crash that leaves me in no doubt that I am unwell. To have no interest in life, move lethargically through the day, and struggle to concentrate on the task in front of me, is entirely out of character.

The future predictions of my natal chart ring true. I would grow up to be utopian in outlook, with great receptivity for beauty, art, and music. I would have a tendency to fall in love quickly and ardently, with a strong erotic compulsion. Marriage was almost certainly on the cards, but my explosive domestic moods would need careful handling if it was to last. There was no doubt that I would be a career woman with a strong sense of vocation. Interestingly from a mental health perspective, my chart cautioned to be wary of drugs: even if medically prescribed, they could have adverse effects.

As a trained researcher, I am open to any method that provides a strong evidence base for decision making, but rather than be guided by astrological predictions throughout my life, I prefer to nurture a strong sense of free will, which, ironically, seems a typically Aries thing to do. Occasionally, I look to astrologers for alternative perspectives and insights, which support navigation of challenging circumstances and significant junctions. More often than not though, I read horoscopes retrospectively, out of curiosity, finding in their high level of accuracy a source of fascination.

I am still lingering beneath the wooden ceiling long after my travel companion has drifted into the great, gleaming hall. I am pondering the four white dragons, which intertwine and hold in place the calendar and sitting figures. They are protecting the nature of reality as taught by the Buddha, symbolising enlightenment. The faintest breeze scuffs my sandled feet, shuffled back from those going to and fro. I am in no hurry, there is nowhere else I need to be. The relative quiet and cool of the North is heavenly after the humidity and bustle of the South, and standing here, at the portal to another way of being, there is a sense of peace that I will revisit for years to come.

TOLERANCE

LAND

I choose to live on an island, the middle of three, because I need the sea and its big wide open. Or perhaps I need the sea because I was born on an island, and it was never a choice. There is an invisible limit to my tolerance for landlock that I measure in drive time. Twenty minutes from home to the coast is as far as I can comfortably stretch. This is a long distance for someone who grew up with sand between her toes, three houses back from the shoreline.

Distance is not the only consideration. Show me a scoop of ocean and I will gauge its power to soothe. Miles of cold grey churn and chop, glaring mean slivers of windswept sand — these offer little solace. I long instead for generous arcs, a string of bays on a clear day, knowing they are there in mist and fog. Bays flanked by grassy cliffs that drop like a gasp to marble blue-green. The bright, white brushstroke of a lighthouse, the lumbering, toddling, swooping company of sea lions, penguins, and albatross. A jewelled path of tiny shells, coned and spiralled beneath my feet.

For a brief time, my limits can be suspended, my landlock tolerance stretched to accommodate a mirror lake, a circle of mountains, an icy river tumbling through gorge. I bargain with myself, for the sake of blazing autumn avenues, white blanket ridges, orchards blossomed pink, and bowlfuls of cherries hanging heavy for poaching, over an empty schoolyard fence. I am steadied by the knowing, that a sea on one side, and an ocean on the other, are only hours away. Without the means to get there though, and without breath-taking distraction, there is a closing in, insufficient air, a low-level buzz of distress that clamours in my head and chest and compels my feet to remedy.

SPACE

My ability to flourish in a city is measured by the time it takes to get out of it, the number of vantage points from which I can see beyond its boundaries, and the size of the canvas of sky above my head, outside my window to drink. My horror of constraint is all encompassing: my breath catches on the closeness of a tunnel, the crawl of gridlock traffic, the coffin of an elevator. I avoid the oppression of obstruction, the possibility of no way out. I walk, and take the stairs. I catch a ferry, from which I could jump and swim. I need space for the sake of space, for the sake of sanity. I need an exit strategy. I cannot focus in a cubicle in a maze of cubicles. I cannot sit calmly in a cluttered room, or share a bed and sleep. I am ill-suited to cohabitation.

BEAUTY

My ability to flourish in a city is measured by the ratio of grey to green, the proportion of aged stone and warm brick to cold concrete and glass, the balance of cobbled lanes whispering stories and sprawling motorways that whine, by how much history has been preserved. Surrounded daily by only the contemporary, the unlovely, I am bereft and unmoored.

Depression is mild but sustained, and can tip the balance, eventually.

I associate man-made beauty with what came before my time, when harmony and longevity, pomp and flair, still had currency. If you lose me in a city, you will find me in the historic precinct, my neck craning to spot gargoyles on a splendid stone facade, eyes straining to read the faded typeface in an old advertisement on the side of a warehouse. I will be standing still in the middle of the footpath, head bowed, studying a commemorative plaque, or halfway up a stairwell, leaning over the banister, gazing at the enamel tiled floor of the entrance way.

You will not be surprised, when you visit my home, to find yourself in another era. You will walk down a generous hallway, through 1930s door frames, beneath pressed ceilings with cameo corners. You will sit down in rooms studded with oak bookshelves, bevelled mirrors, faded velvet chairs, and hairline cracked china, and say, Oh, it's very you.

ORDER

You do, like others, wonder at the imposition of order, and ask if my house is always this tidy. I smile assent, but do not say, it cannot be any other way. I cannot abide a desk off centre, the unflattering angle of a vase, a dented cushion, a folded blanket misaligned, a picture frame too far to the left, the uneven drop of a quilt, an imbalance of books on shelves. I will never tell you that I even consider the angle of an open door, that I am compelled to order everything within my reach.

In an earlier era, you may not have believed that I do this for myself, and not for you — I do, after all, come from a line of house-proud women. Now, in the age of no expectations and not enough time, no such keeping up appearances, such precision is unnerving. I suspect that, sadly, it is precisely because you never see a forgotten tea-ringed cup, a splayed open book, or a cardigan on the floor, that you don't return my invitation, and so I never see your home or know you as well as I would like. Perhaps, if you noticed instead the paintings in every room, you might see that my obsessive eye for line and balance and energy and colour is artistic, and not a cause for disquiet.

LIGHT

We all have, I suppose, our own design parameters within which we operate and perform, limits to the sensory and psychic loads that we can comfortably tolerate. Generally, those around me seem less particular, less sensitive, and oblivious or indifferent to environments in which I struggle to cope. For decades, I willed myself to endure sub-optimal conditions, in an unsuccessful effort to cultivate tolerance and normality, cultivating instead a pattern of frustration, distress and desertion. My childhood fondness for the story of the *The Princess and the Pea*, and my early fascination with Platonic idealism was telling: the extraordinary tendency to be bruised black and blue by the fly in the ointment, and a philosophy of perfection, are a foolproof combination for suffering.

As a gardener, I take pains to understand ideal conditions for planting, and optimal care throughout the seasons. I attend to soil and space, timing and temperature, companionship. I have a special affection for plants that flourish in the soft, filtered light of woodlands: bluebells, primroses, foxgloves, snowdrops, winter roses. I too, shy away from harsh extremities; the naked assault of office strip lights, curtains pulled to blackout during the day, make me instantly cross. Fiercely loyal to natural light, I dim blazing bulbs whenever I can, thankful for small mercies.

TEMPERATURE

I grew up in the north of New Zealand's North Island, on a narrow stretch of land, six hours drive from the Cape at the tip, give or take. Seasons in the sub-tropics are much of a muchness, temperature ranges moderate and days mostly mild. For me, it was the high humidity that most distinguished summer from winter, and what was once home from those further south, the sticky oppression that hits me like a wall, wringing me out when I step off the plane to visit. Breathing full the fresh chill of autumn and leaves on the turn, pulling on my navy school jumper, was always a relief.

Now, settled in the south of the South, where seasons are clearly colour-coded green, orange, white, and pink, I take pleasure in dressing for the weather. Relishing the close comfort of a merino wool skivvy, the satisfying hang of heavy winter trousers, the warm wrap of thick, knitted scarves that fall to my knees, and the flash of a bright beret, I feel cheated when, walking into over-heated offices, I flush irritable within minutes. Stripping off layers, I grumble and question no-one in particular: How can you stand it? Others, not bothered, wearing the same cotton shirts throughout the year, shrug and keep working. I steer clear of iron radiators, and defiantly push open a window.

SOUND

I choose to live on the lush green flat of a quiet valley, beyond the tolerable hum of a small city. It is hard to believe that I could once endure the predictable 3:00 a.m. crash of binned glass below an apartment, or the drone of a television through the wall. It has always been impossible to understand how anyone can bear the daily scream and squeal and howl and whine of children and their toys, the thump and rage of teenagers' music, the irritating pop and chatter of background radio, or the sustained generic groan of motorway traffic within earshot of home. There have been places where the clang of scaffolding and temporary barrage of construction outside has permanently driven me to a new address.

Now, it is morning, the back door propped open to the faint babbling and streaming of river tributaries, and tui conducting the melodic dawn chorus. Later, the contented pulse of bees beneath my bedroom window, and if I'm lucky, the familial chatter of river ducks waddling down the path, or the leisurely clop of horse hooves past the front door. Evening calls of neighbouring sheep travel to the north-facing bay window, where I sit watching the play of fading light on the protective flanks of the hills. Sleep, when darkness settles, is unbroken by the creaking, elderly bones of the house.

It is in this place that I live and work alone, in a permanent state of retreat, soaking my exhausted brain in merciful calm. Over time, worn down by annual upheaval, this high ratio of silence and soothe to intrusive, amplified sound has become essential, an item at the top of a list that defines the parameters of suitable real estate.

Hypersensitivity and intense emotion are two ends of a rope that can trip me up, and tie me in the same old useless knots, and yet, rope, of course, can also be enabling. It is no hardship to mimic the lilt of language, or coordinate my feet with the travel of music. It does not pain me to catch a piano note off key. I am not sorry to have been stopped in my tracks on a warm spring night, at once rooted to the spot, and exquisitely uplifted by strains of opera through the windows of a theatre.

TIME

If we are living in an age of not enough time, I have always had it in spades, protecting it fiercely from the tiresome, the mediocre, the inauthentic, to feast on the exhilarating, the excellent, the unique. Infamously impatient, possessed by efficiency, and intolerant of incompetence, it is entrenched politeness when I nod and smile at people who waste my time. I do not seek company for the sake of company. I am quick to prune interactions that don't enrich the soil in which I stand. I see people as ingredients, forces of creativity, and the servants of art; those who can be enjoyed raw are rare.

ENERGY

Each time we meet, I attune to your energy and pay close attention. I notice your posture and pace, the persuasion of your smile. I see your attempt to contain, or willingness to expand and overflow. If the colour in your cheeks suggests health or fluster, if your tone of voice tells me you want to be anywhere but here, doing anything but this, how much of your attention is with me — I catch all of these things. You know that I notice, because I tell you something of what I see.

My focus is unwavering. I listen closely to what you do and do not say. I hear if you are contradicting or trying to convince yourself, and mark the moments when you curate the truth for my hearing. I edit and proofread your script.

It feels to me as if I am sitting at the core of you, but the accuracy of my location is never certain. Some of what you don't say I carry with me when we part: the self-defence beneath your gentle deflections, the hopelessness of no way out behind your wide-eyed stare, confusion from a lack of self-awareness, the paralysis of fear. It may add to the weight of a necklace of sinkers that pulls me under on a heavy day, and I may need time to resurface and settle, but this is how I experience meaningful connection.

When we meet in a group, it is difficult for me to attend. Multiple energies collide, scatter, spin off and blur, our language muddied with dishonesty and trivia. Our noise sounds to me like the crackle and hiss of a bad telephone line, like I'm missing every second word, and we're not really here at all. The more our presence is diluted by others, the more frustrated and exhausted I will be. A party, a crowd, is avoided at all costs.

DRINK

These days, without the crutch of a fragile stem of a glass half full, and the mellow sway of fermented grape, I am disarmed and exposed. My middle-aged liver can no longer tolerate the blissful dulling that descends, and so until I discover the prop of natural sedation, I must tolerate everything else: the manifold energies and collective noise of a crowd, glaring downlights and overheated rooms, desolate views of concrete and car parks, precious time sacrificed to interruption and incompetence. Steeped in this cocktail of irritants, suspending sensory overwhelm and social anxiety, I am expected to smile and engage, inform and impress, and so I do. Returning home, drained and cross, I fill a tall glass with sparkling water and a squeezed wedge of lemon, which just doesn't cut it.

JOY IS NOT NEGOTIABLE

The gallery hang is so perfect that it snatches her breath and pins her to the doorway. It's as if she is standing on the threshold of a vault: three small rooms of unknown paintings, spotlit on walls of the deepest, richest purple. In a clever trick of curation, a tired antique armchair catches her eye, and invites her in. Impossible to resist, her hand reaches out to years of wood stroked smooth, taking a moment to orient herself in the bejewelled space.

In the room to her right, bright square pockets of distinctly Dunedin garden reduce her to the size of a pansy, a viola, the lowliest forget-me-not. Immersed in jungles of lush, domestic foliage, she feasts on a palette of blues, veronica starring, orange gerberas flashing defiant. Drawing closer, she absorbs the quiet of cornflowers and the comfort of columbines — mutual friends from gardens past. Raising her eyes, a bold, purple iris is duelling for supremacy over a grand tulip the imperial hue of the gallery walls.

Seed heads, deadheads, dandelion — the paintings are indiscriminate. When she tips her head to a falling gladiolus, and can't satisfy her gardener's instinct to stake the poor plant, she wants to turn the painting the right way up. To witness without correcting, such a gift, an invitation to another way of seeing. The generosity of the artist, the openness of the viewer: this is not a trivial exchange.

Blossom-drunk, she drifts through the central space, looking past her indifference to indifferent cats, past storybook state houses, to the familiar and beloved arcs of green that frame the city and meet the southern sky. Looking past wilted flowers in white Crown Lynn vases, she delights in two-dimensional, mid-century wallpaper in floral and pinstripe. In the middle of the gallery, she stands in stillness with *Tree*, enveloped by its church of muted greens and dappled light.

On the other side of the gallery, in a pastel box of bust portraits, she meets the painter's people. Life-size, no-nonsense faces, dour sitters in no-fuss attire, carving out rectangles of block colour. Roaming the room, fascinated by family resemblance, she is suddenly arrested by a dapper young man with an air of performance and the hands of a musician, dressed to the nines. *Ben, An Artist's Son*, is so splendid in his gold waistcoat, red jacket, and slicked back hair, so self-possessed, she spends her final moments basking in his youthful radiance until — bursting with joy — she floats out the door, down the stairs, and out into the rain.

If only she had floated right out into the rain, but euphoria has taken hold and she can't get enough, so she floats out the door, down the stairs, and into the gift shop. She wants to bottle this moment, own this rapture, in any shape or form, at any price — she will have need of it again. Never mind that only yesterday, she gave herself a stern talking to, after weeks of must-haves and just-one-more, and taken pains to reduce expenses. Joy is not negotiable.

It's too easy, she is so elated, it seems that just about anything might summon this particular magic, simply by being within reach, right here, right now. The monographs on the slim wooden shelves, the glossy museum press books displayed in the entrance way, the printed exhibition cards on the counter, the bright posters jostling companionably in boxes at her feet. If only she could browse quietly, ground herself, but she chats distractedly to the woman sitting at the counter, who — aggressively pierced and dressed for a punk performance — covets her Mary Poppins carpet bag. Fondling dust jackets, sifting through cards, committing herself with every audible declaration of appreciation and desire, she builds a nest of treasures on an oversized red armchair until she exhausts all possibilities.

The price of exuberance paid, her arms barely wrapping around her loot, she struggles out the door into the rain, drops her car keys in the middle of the road when her tower threatens to topple, and collapses into the driver's seat, victorious. But her heart is still soaring, her mind still racing — how else might she sustain this joyous note, this music of the soul?

On the drive home — the glow of her purchases already fading — she is struck by the idea that she might somehow belong to the very place itself, and other places like it. She strides through her front door and sits, pinned to her sofa, until she has become a member, and signed herself up to news of every gallery, museum, festival and venue for arts and cultural heritage in the city. There. Her plate, for today at least, is full.

She should know by now — from every new place, every fresh start — that it will be too much, that the constant stream of announcements and invitations and newsletters will overwhelm her. She will tire of small talk with strangers over wine and cheese and cups of tea, and wish herself home in her pyjamas with a book. She will resent the requests to volunteer, to organise, to stretch her time. The sense of connection will become suffocating. She will cancel, withdraw, unsubscribe. She will wonder whatever possessed her.

25 DECEMBER

1 DECEMBER

More than a dozen freshly cut Christmas trees lean against the low wall of old red brick, still tip-spangled from last night's rain. What luck, to be the only customer in sight: she can savour the moment she looks forward to all year without the bustle of over-excited children and time-poor parents. A bored attendant in faded t-shirt and worn jeans hovers, ready to help load her small car parked on the kerb. If only he would stop interrupting her decision-making with his friendly chatter; tree height has determined her shortlist, but now she's finding it hard to choose.

Why anyone would prefer to haul a crude and ugly fake from a garage each year, or dust off an ultra-modern nod to a tree, when they might enjoy the real thing so affordably is beyond her. Better to go without completely, as she has done so often in the past, decorating the door handles and bare surfaces of her tiny apartments instead.

The slim, elegant branches of the most unusual tree in the line-up win out over the heavy-scented fullness of its more typical neighbours. Its grey-green arms, reaching for the sky, hold out thumbelina pinecones like offerings. When the tree takes pride of place in front of her mantelpiece, it appears so like an enchanted sculpture that it's almost tempting to leave it unadorned, but to miss out on the annual reunion with her treasured decorations would be an unimaginable break with tradition.

2 DECEMBER

Beside the tree, a collection of small boxes has been ceremoniously laid on the floor by a middle-aged child at play. The unwrapping of most objects she anticipates; a few, almost forgotten, she greets with delighted surprise. Until recently, her collection of decorations has differed in size and shape most years, swept through the revolving door of relentless relocation with the rest of her possessions. Only a favoured few have survived the decades, the rest joining the raft of charity shop donations as she up sticks to reinvent herself.

Cross-legged on the rug, she gently unpacks the longest serving. The clumsily sequinned, miniature felt stocking, sewn by hand with beginner blanket stitch as snow fell on the playground of her London primary school. The slightly battered candle, crafted from toilet roll and yellow cellophane, its hand-drawn paper flame still flickering after forty years. Together, they established her quirky theme of fabric and paper, distinguishing her Christmas tree from the tinsel glitz and plastic kitsch common to department stores and so many homescapes in December.

As they emerge from boxes and tissue, she greets them each in turn, grateful that her playthings have survived the always unpredictable journey of the past year. Pearl-headed paper angels in yellow concertina robes, and green quilted stars. Stuffed felt puddings and tartan cotton robins. Musical scores replayed for baby bunting, and recycled ribbon bow ties. A handful of heritage buttons — precious inheritance from her Nana's dressmaking drawers — crafted into hanging baubles. She permits a single string of fairy lights, and a lengthy featherweight necklace of red, to pull it all together.

The rest of the house she leaves for last, placing the blue china angel on the side table in the hall, her mother's worn book of carols and childhood figurines on the piano. The wicker wreath attends the door, and her large woollen stocking, from the era of the paper candle, guards the fireplace. Extra decorations loop the doorknobs, and her much-loved advent calendars are propped on the mantels. As her Christmas carol playlist cycles through the heavenly choirs of Oxbridge, she stands back to admire her handiwork and declare The Tree done.

3 DECEMBER

In the dining room, a quaint still-life awaits her at the end of the long oak table: a small stack of cards and envelopes, a scribbled list and address book, a worthy pen, and a sleeve of stamps commemorating the Queen. Will this year's Victoriana scene be considered so lovely that recipients recycle her card annually as a decoration? Wanting to preserve the endangered custom of printed cards at Christmas, she hopes so.

The flurry of cards once received at this time of year has steadily dwindled to a few through her cobwebbed letter box. The cost of postage is becoming prohibitive, and mail can take weeks to reach family across the sea, but she won't be deprived of this pleasure. The more fleeting good wishes she receives by contemporary methods, the more she longs for the slow consideration of calligraphy. Moving the fruit bowl and candlesticks aside, she sits down and begins.

4 DECEMBER

A mug of black tea, sitting in a shaft of sunlight, steams beside this year's literary companion: a first edition in navy blue cloth, a white garland of snowdrops, snowflakes, mistletoe, and holly stamped on its boards. *Christmas Days* by Jeanette Winterson had been a thrilling purchase on a recent road trip sprinkled with secondhand bookshops — a surprising discovery as she crouched down with the end of the alphabet in a quiet aisle of fiction.

The now-and-again book club at her local bookshop has Charles Dickens covered with its annual celebration. Her mouth is already watering at the thought of nibbling on quince tarts, and diving into homemade plum pudding with brandy butter, as she listens to a reading from the *Christmas Carol*. Surrounded by fellow book lovers, she will not be alone in her suspension of disbelief, when the Antipodean summer sun begins to fade the window display, and swelter the crowded room.

6 DECEMBER

With her final book purchases complete, it is time for The Wrapping (always more fun than The Unwrapping, with its weighty potential for disappointment and awkward gratitude). She is kneeling before the tree, surrounded by long rolls of printed paper, sellotape, scissors, and string, rummaging for the handful of name tags she is certain must be somewhere in her box of cards.

Today's official ceremony is slightly undermined by the realities of international parcel post, which requires her to send presents to family overseas by late November. With these already dispatched, she has found new ways to ensure her tree is not bereft of company in December. Two piles of books, thoughtfully gathered throughout the year from fairs and charity shops, are fodder for a literary lucky dip for her friends. Now, all that remains to do is convert these to surprise, with cheerful paper, clean edges, neat corners, and suitably smart bow ties.

9 DECEMBER

Ingredients for fruit cake, mince tarts, and orange and grapefruit marmalade are tucked and stacked about the old galley kitchen. Her finger-smeared recipe book is propped in waiting on the counter, behind an enamel bowl of eggs. Baking tins sit patiently on the tired oven, cooling their heels until the next slather of butter. Glass jars with red and white gingham lids squat in the roasting pan. All are ready to be magicked into Christmas treats for friends close by — homemade presents, along with books, being her favourite to give and receive.

The humblest kitchen utensils empower her to defy space and time, the handling of measuring cup and wooden spoon summoning the presence of her mother miles away, her grandmothers now gone. Embracing tradition but not bound to it, she forgives herself the shortcuts, and reaches for the blender. She prefers her marmalade hand-cut, but she has left The Baking a little late this year.

10 DECEMBER

The chill of the white stone cathedral belies the mild evening outside, but she is content to sit in her winter coat for the pleasure of angelic sopranos. Seated alone and near the front, doing her best to pretend she is the only one in the audience, she basks in the kaleidoscope of stained-glass windows, and the scent of pews oiled to a shine, waiting for the carols to begin.

She is trying to ignore the gossip and fidgets of the waiting crowd behind her, but someone near the back has seen fit to bring a mewling baby, which she considers ironically inappropriate. If the child isn't taken outside to settle, her evening of carols is doomed: she can already feel her blood boiling, her eyes seeing red, her brain pressing against her skull. In this place of peace and goodwill, she has, in response to a few bleats from an infant, become a cliché of combustible intolerance.

Instinctively, she sits on the aisle at any event, making for an easier exit at such moments. Her attachment to courtesy, and sensitivity to sound, simply won't permit her to endure the real or anticipated threat of unwelcome interruption: the tension in her body escalates so fast that she can become a powder keg set to blow within minutes. As the choir files in before her, and the audience babble subsides, she can already feel her enjoyment of this beautiful place draining away.

16 DECEMBER

The Farmer's Market is busier than usual at this time of the morning, with many getting a jump-start on their Christmas stockpiling. The concrete car park next to the old gingerbread railway station has transformed into a cheerful bazaar, jostling to the grind of coffee beans, and the tune of Jingle Bells by a local brass band. She could load the jute grocery bag slung over her arm in ten minutes, but she comes here rarely, and prefers to take her time.

In contrast to the necessities that routinely fill her supermarket trolley, visits to the market are all about what she wants, not what she needs. Today, she wants ready-to-burst Central Otago cherries and soft, succulent apricots. She desires sticky wedges of Evansdale cheese, and a slim column of lemon-infused olive oil.

Further along the raised concourse, she bags a flaky Turkish pastry stuffed with spinach and feta, a perfect Portuguese custard tart, and a jarred dollop of fresh salmon pâté. Her bag is soon brimming, and her pocket money blown, but she can't resist filling her hands on the way out: a Cornish pastie for second breakfast, and a slice of frangipane tart for afternoon tea.

24 DECEMBER

A busy fortnight of holiday farewells to friends and colleagues descends into stillness on Christmas Eve. A cup of chamomile brews on the table to the left of her armchair, as she watches the fairy lights skim the surfaces of the few remaining presents at the base of the tree — some sent by family, and a few she has chosen for herself. Queen's College choir is singing the Coventry Carol, filling her eyes with tears, as the familiar dread starts taking over.

The joys of December have come to an end. She has tried so many times, in so many ways, to release the ties of tradition at this moment, like an apron no longer required. To convince her family that for her, tomorrow is just a normal day, that she prefers to potter about happily as usual without fuss and fanfare, and be left in peace. She is done with the pressure of performance, and so she chooses to spend it alone. They are not convinced, and neither, perhaps, is she.

Her happy childhood memories of family gatherings have been swamped by those more recent: breakdowns, break-ups, broken glass. All efforts to distract herself on the surface — with friends, camping, even a random church service — have failed to triumph over the same day beneath. After a morning of summoning false cheer to field family phone calls, she will endure wracking guilt and piercing, conditioned loneliness, as she rides out the pain of Christmases past that run on an unremitting loop until the day is over.

26 DECEMBER

She wakes on Boxing Day with relief, as the early morning sun lights up the edges of a heavy velvet curtain the colour of the sea. With Christmas over, and no expectations, she stretches her limbs in eager anticipation of the summer's day and approaching new year. Cherries and apricots for breakfast. A stroll on the beach. Short stories in the garden, under the shade of the cherry tree. This evening, she will pack her decorations into their small boxes. Perhaps, she will be able to let them linger a little longer next year.

RÉSUMÉ REVISED

Name: #1
　　Address: #36
　　Website: #6

PROFILE

In Life Before Diagnosis, when I freely overflowed with passion, I would have started my professional profile with the relevant thing that I was passionate about: books, learning, languages, heritage, the arts. It was a way of introducing myself as an ideal candidate — passion for one's work being generally associated with positive outcomes. My career, for the most part, has been seeded and saved by passion; even in the midst of damage control, when I was losing my mind and losing my way, I could always tap into another source of passion to steer me through the professional wreckage into calmer, clearer waters.

When I discovered that my passion for literature did not extend to the rigmarole of academia, I became a rare book dealer. When I fled from the promised land of book publishing, my love of languages opened new doors. Later, my passion for cultural heritage fuelled a second attempt at academia. When I was stretchered off the field for being too practical, I channelled my practicality into crowdfunding for the arts.

On paper, my career is more varied than most, but I pitch it as logical, strategic. Sitting across from prospective employers, I explain that my career has evolved alongside technology — a tidy version of the truth. I have even tailored my pitch to inspire Humanities graduates, extolling the virtues of a career jungle gym in lieu of a ladder — each sideways stretch an opportunity to *broaden, upskill, refocus,* or *apply*. At the time, I spoke in reverent tones of *enhancing employability*. I didn't sell it as a story of survival, or a cautionary tale about the erosion of a creative soul.

I was an early exponent of Lean principles: rapid phases of experimentation and failing fast naturally aligning with the relentless rollercoaster that no one, least of all me, had recognised as bipolar. What friends observed as bravery was largely frustration and distress converted at high speed to fearlessness. I used to be baffled by the tenacity of people who stayed in their lane, which I scorned as a lack of curiosity and ambition. These days, I am envious, but for as long as I was serving the humanities, I rolled with each reinvention.

I loved the buzz of a personal rebrand, and the blemish-free canvas of a new website. Riding the confluence of hypomania and the empowering rush of a new domain, I relished the creative flurry of choosing a new design theme, breathed full the fresh air of a new profile. With these tools I conjured a bridge between the old me and the new, as I sprinted to turn the page to the next chapter. Inspired by my bold and frequent pivots, and persuaded by my positive spin, friends suggested I could be a life coach.

For over two decades, I took it for granted that my passion was a bottomless well, so it was surprising and sickening when the bucket scraped the bottom and came up empty. So many years of dream-job disillusion and abandonment had finally limited my options, and run my enthusiasm into the ground. Over time, passion had been diluted to interest, interest diluted to ability. A passion for learning became an interest in university management, became an ability to analyse operational data. A passion for writing and publishing became an ability to produce business cases and annual reports. When my work became completely unhooked from the humanities, like a train carriage derailed by tired machinery after years of quick and questionable fixes, I became someone I barely recognised and no longer trusted to see the way forward.

Finding myself in Life After with all passion spent, I need to begin my résumé another way. I could start instead by telling you about the type of role in which I thrive. I could lightly lift words from your job description, and breathe life into their synonyms. I could take a handful of words like *enable* and *optimise*, and gently sow them back into the soil of your vacancy. It sounds calculating, but I will stand by these words so wholeheartedly that if I cannot, for any reason, promptly *enable* or *optimise*, I will not thrive; it will feel as if I have breached a contract with myself. Perhaps, I should hold fast to words that are more reliable — *dynamic, data-oriented, evidence-based* —, adjectives holding less promise than verbs.

KEY SKILLS

Compared with the tricky business of passion, summarising my relevant knowledge, skills and experience is child's play. With a whole attic of career dress-up boxes to choose from, a simple rummage is all it takes. Watch me lay before you an appropriate selection of props in sharp, glinting paragraphs, or a crafted array of verb-speared bullet points.

If I am required to *investigate, evaluate, analyse* and *interpret*, I can do all of these things. If you need me to *engage, build, define, develop, implement* or *manage*, I can do these too. I will add flourishes like *leverage* and *holistic approach*. I will convince us both that there is nothing else I would rather do, that my work to date has led to this point. Given the opportunity, I will even do an applaudable job, until I encounter an inter-personal battle or a large-scale injustice, when my props will not be strong enough to protect me from my fury.

ATTRIBUTES

Allow me to summarise my attributes in suitable tones, worn smooth by dependability and long use. You will learn that I am *focused, organised* and *a reliable team member*. You will discover that I *work confidently across organisations*, and can *shift seamlessly between big picture thinking and fine detail*. Because this is the truth, you will never suspect how I prefer to spend my days: still, silent, in solitude, like a monk or medieval scribe, filling pages with words, following the light.

PROFESSIONAL EXPERIENCE

In the neat outline of my professional experience, the bold font of job titles, and familiarity of established employers will divert your attention from locations and periods of time. Skim-reading at pace, in your efforts to short-list, it's safe to assume that you will not read between the lines or ponder my associated abilities. After all, I am not applying to relocate you to another part of the country, or the other side of the world. You do not need to know that I have lived in more places than there were years to live in them. You do not need to know that I have mastered the art of packing a box, making a home, rebuilding a life. Let it suffice that I am *versatile* and *quick to adapt to new environments*.

PROFESSIONAL DEVELOPMENT

Given my tendency to bounce and bend, reinvent and spin, it is not surprising that I am drawn to the intangible arts of Agile and Change Management. If not to your taste, perhaps my dusty development efforts in Project Planning provide more assurance. Either way, I should not mislead you, since learning and doing can be different things.

I am best applied at the beginning and the end, where I can play in the frameworks with well-intentioned words. I have no stomach or stamina for the in-between, the realities of delay, compromise, incompetence, disappointment. I can evaluate the present, identify opportunities for improvement. I can paint a picture of the future, scope the land and mark it out. When it has been built I can assess its impact. While I can pour concrete, erect scaffolding, wield a hammer, and drive a nail, there are others better suited to the job.

QUALIFICATIONS

My formal qualifications, once sharp and bright with promise, are now faded and soft-edged with handling, like a stack of tarot cards. As evidence of my intentions, and ability to reinterpret, they have proven infinitely flexible, but it pains me each time I shuffle.

Here: The Bachelor of Arts, enthroned and attended by English Literature and Art History. I bow my head, humbled by my disrupted efforts to serve as teacher, writer, painter, champion. Here: The Diploma, carried by a young Page in belted tunic, the beginning of my thwarted journey as book editor.

Next: Honours, standing determined in red robe, magicking an inspired pathway out of the professional wilderness with Digital Humanities. Honours is followed by a chariot: The Master, a manager of information standing firm in polished armour, and readiness to play mercenary in the battles of employment.

Finally, the card I hold to my chest: reversed Fortitude, woman and lion hanging in mid-air, the almost-but-not-quite PhD. Only those who look closely will see its shadow in the job title Researcher, the desertion of a three-year down payment of passion and time.

RECOMMENDATIONS

It is astonishing, each time I look back at what I see as professional devastation, and turn to salt, that employers have vouched for me so generously. My résumé is lifted high by testimonials as if by the voices of angels. They sing creative, talented, dedicated, efficient, outstanding. I contribute tangible value, I set the bar. My boisterous, opinionated self is considered an *exceptional communicator*. Incredibly, I have been at once a person unable to conquer self-sabotage, and *someone you can depend on and trust with anything precious to you*. I can, evidently, be on my knees and gasping for air, panic-stricken with perceived failure and desperate to disappear, and still not let you down.

NOTES FOR REVISION

Now that I have said all the things I cannot say, it is time for yet another revision. Exhausted, and feeling trapped by design and circumstance, I cannot, for the first time, face it alone. I surrender to the determined positivity of a career coach, and lean into her painful, probing questions.

She asks for context, with the caveat that she is coach not counsellor. She encourages me to frame my most upsetting experiences and regrettable decisions as "plot twists". I latch onto her frameworks and step-by-step guidance. I set myself homework, dicing values into spreadsheets to self-soothe, and notice how the revelation of diagnosis has imposed new priorities.

Each time we regroup, our two heads buzzing in a tiny virtual box, we play the game of quick-fire analysis like the skilled professionals we are. Not wanting to make her uncomfortable, I am smiling, laughing, articulate, constructive. I forgive her for not sensing my desperation, as I work to excavate a professional that I can only hope has been buried alive.

INSTRUCTIONS FOR BIPOLAR

Diagnosis is not a cure. You've been here before, and you'll likely be here again, but you know how to get through this. Let me remind you — we'll take it one step at a time.

INSTRUCTIONS FOR HYPOMANIA

You are overwhelmed with emotion about something that you want to run from or towards at full tilt. Probably, you're distressed, and you want to quit work, reinvent yourself, and relocate (again) — it seems easier to run than endure these feelings. Perhaps you're in love, and you're compelled to do whatever you think it takes to make everything perfect. Either way, you're prepared to abandon life as you know it.

You've felt like this before, but you're telling yourself the circumstances are different this time, exceptional. You think you need to take action immediately — you don't. You can only see one way forward, but there is never only one way forward. You need to slow down.

If you're rapidly making plans to radically change your life, you're really high. Start taking magnesium to calm you down, and hold fast to your routine like it's a life raft.

Your stomach is in knots and you've lost your appetite. Eat anyway. Keep it simple.

You're finding it hard to sleep. Your brain is racing, and you're probably filling a notebook with ideas at high speed. Get up, make a piece of toast with honey and a cup of sedating tea, then go back to bed. Apply lavender oil to your pulse points. Listen to gentle music. Count slowly, breathe deep.

Tell someone you trust. You both know what is happening now. Name it: this is hypomania. Saying it aloud will help to hold you accountable for managing it.

You cannot stabilise your mood until you process what has triggered you. You know what it is: your bipolar episodes are never random. You need to sit with it, unpack it, defuse its power. Get out your journal, and write it down.

Channel your excess energy in ways that won't over-stimulate you: write a story, paint a canvas, practice piano, tackle your list of chores.

———

Be mindful of your surroundings, and focus on the task in front of you. Narrate your actions, one step at a time.

———

Keep socialising to a minimum: conversation will over-stimulate you. You will talk too much and say things you will regret. You need to stay calm.

———

Don't commit your time to any new initiatives, no matter how excited you are right now. It will be too much for you later, I promise.

———

Make a list of anything unusual you desperately want to buy. If you still want it when this episode has passed, it will still be there. This is hard, I know. You will obsess about this purchase, convinced you need it for your new life, but it will lose its allure as soon as you own it. You don't need to buy stuff, you need to buy time. Slow. Down.

INSTRUCTIONS FOR DEPRESSION

You have been overwhelmed by despair and can see no way through. When you feel like crying, your instinct is to suppress sadness and maintain a semblance of control. You're afraid that if you start you won't be able to stop. Let go. Crying is an important part of processing, and you always feel calmer afterwards.

It's no wonder that your brain, if left unchecked, chooses to run with hypomania over this: depression is unacceptable. Your brain feels inflamed, as if it's pressing against your skull.

There are people who can support you, but talking and listening for any length of time is difficult and gives you a headache. Check in with friends and family, but explain you need to keep it brief.

You cannot recover until you process what is distressing you. You know what it is: your bipolar episodes are never random. Sit with it, unpack it, defuse its power. Write it down.

You usually pride yourself on your attention to detail, but now you make mistakes. You skip letters when writing, and struggle to summon simple words. Your beautiful handwriting has become scrawl. Don't worry. It's your journal — no one reads it. Keep writing.

Your working memory is floundering, and you forget why you've gone into a room. This is upsetting, but speak kindly to yourself. Talking aloud maintains your focus, but makes you feel like a crazy person — just do what you have to do.

———

Hand-eye coordination makes you feel nauseous. Simple tasks like cleaning the house and tending the garden are too difficult. Playing the piano is a no-go. This is frustrating, but it's temporary. Listen to the music of others. The rest can wait.

———

You've lost your appetite and your pleasure in cooking, but this will pass. Keep things simple. There are tins of soup in the pantry for times like this. Remind yourself how good a peanut butter sandwich tastes.

———

If you're very unwell, your concentration is shot, and driving is a risk. This is temporary. You don't need to travel far right now, and your favourite spots will still be there later. Relax. You live in a beautiful place. Go for a walk.

———

If you're very unwell, you're struggling to read, but there are always stories. Your favourite children's books are next to your bed for this reason. If these make your head hurt, choose a book with pictures. You don't need to go to the library — your house is like a bookshop — how cool is that? Maybe you can't read anything. Don't panic. This will pass. Watch a film instead.

———

You're going to bed early at night like a small child, and dragging yourself out of bed in the morning like an old woman. You're tired all the time. You could sit and stare out the window for hours, but you don't want to be a mental illness cliché. It does no harm to sit and stare for a while. Be still.

There will be social commitments you feel obliged to keep. If an event requires anything more than turning up and sitting in silence, it is going to be too much for you. If you push yourself it will undermine your recovery. You're not well. Say so. You believe that others will think you pathetic, but this is not helpful. You'll never know what they really think, and it doesn't matter anyway. Tend to yourself.

There is always work to do, and tasks you usually complete with ease feel like heavy lifting. You're conserving your energy and rallying to protect your income, but it's exhausting. No one seems to have noticed: people still think your work is great. You wonder, not for the first time, if it's possible that a pace that feels painfully slow to you is actually within the bounds of normal productivity. All the same, if you have been pushing yourself through mental sludge for weeks, it's time to take a break. You're the boss now, so be a kind one.

You feel disconnected from everything around you. Without the ability to feel joy in the things you love, or satisfaction in the things you do well, you lose your sense of agency, identity. You are buried by bland, colourless illness: stock standard, off-the-shelf depression. This will pass. You haven't disappeared. Check in with the bipolar community. If you can, read a bipolar memoir or a blog, watch a documentary — you will feel less alone.

You've been depressed so long that it's starting to feel normal. It isn't. When you are out the other side, it will amaze you that you could be so ill. You're doing all the right things to get through this. I'm so proud of you.

Connect with your body to get out of your head. Go outside and sit in the sun. Roll out your yoga mat. Put on some music, and dance in your living room. You won't feel like doing this, but do it anyway. Trust me.

Your mood will improve before your brain function recovers. You'll think you're ready to return to your usual pace, but you need more time. Multi-tasking is not your friend right now, and will only make you feel unwell. Rest a little longer.

Maybe external circumstances change, or someone explains something in a way that changes your perspective. Perhaps you'll have a dream that gives you strength, and something inside you shifts. Suddenly, your mind is set free. It feels as if a storm has passed and the sky has cleared. You notice light, warmth, colour. Your senses return to normal. Like magic, you feel like yourself again: focused, optimistic, energised.

As you rush about, catching up on life, you may pause for a moment and grieve for the time you have lost to bipolar. It feels like you spend half your life wrangling this illness, which is true. Let yourself cry. Now, onward.

INSTRUCTIONS FOR EUTHYMIA

Now that you've returned to what you think of as steady state, it's hard to believe you have been so unwell.

You're tired of being a person with a mental illness. Maintaining constant vigilance is a chore. Now that you feel so much better, you're tempted to think that everything you do to proactively manage bipolar is negotiable: avoidance of stress; strict adherence to a supportive routine; commitment to a life of simplicity, solitude, and silence. For as long as you suffer with this illness, it isn't negotiable.

Your daily monitoring of sleep, stress, energy, brain function, mood, headaches, and magnesium dosage seems obsessive, but this information helps others help you. It takes you no more than a minute each day — keep it up.

You don't like taking medication of any kind, even natural supplements — they make you feel like a sick person. You would rather spend that money on something else, something inspiring, like books. Vitamin D and fish oil are boring. Keep taking them. Your brain is amazing, but it needs all the help it can get.

Everyone has health challenges, and this is yours. You have everything you need to survive, so do what you have to do.

In the two years since diagnosis, you have sustained self-employment, created a home, planted a garden, nurtured new friendships, and contributed to your community. You have sat down each morning, five days a week, and written a book to this point. You've got this.

SUMMIT BID

STANDARD TREATMENT

As I unwind my long woollen scarf in the chilly hallway, still sobbing and reeling from what feels like professional malpractice, my phone receives a message from the office in which the tears began. I take it into my front room to read, where a midday wedge of winter sun is warming the dark oak rocking chair. According to the description of service in the invoice attached, I have just received a Standard Consultation and Treatment. If I wasn't so furious, I would laugh out loud.

The sender of the invoice is a clinical psychologist I had chosen with care, who claims to specialise in mood disorders and associated methods of talking therapy — a form of standard treatment for people with bipolar. She had agreed to meet in response to my request for ongoing support, which I have been deferring for two years.

With avoidance as my default strategy for stability, I am living a half-life. I am acutely aware of the three-fold suffering that I associate with confrontation: the dread of emotional meltdown, the actual meltdown, and the frustration and shame that follows. Having recently admitted to myself that I might cope better with professional help, I was fully prepared to invest time, effort, and money into establishing a trusting connection.

I had anticipated that we might not "click" immediately or at all, but I had not expected carelessness bordering on cruelty. In less than an hour, this alleged expert has destroyed my tenuous faith in psychotherapy, and made my previous experience, with a useless, parroting counterpart at the other end of town, look like a holiday snapshot in comparison.

The money required to pay for said service, which has done more harm than good, could be spent instead on any number of things of benefit to me. Six months of nutritional supplements, or four months of swimming pool membership. Four doctor's visits, or two massages. I could cover the annual cost of my phone plan, heat my house for a month in mid-winter, or fill my supermarket trolley with groceries for a fortnight. If I tasked a plumber to fix my cracked spouting, I wouldn't pay for them to leave it in a worse state. It's tempting to bin the invoice.

I head for the kitchen at the far end of the house, in desperate need of something to calm me down. While the kettle is boiling for valerian tea, I duck into the bedroom to swap shoes for slippers, and town clothes for more warmth and comfort, rattled and fuming with every step. I'm kicking myself for throwing good money after bad, but it's not just about the money.

I'm grieving for the time and emotional energy wasted on the build up, sufferance, and fall out associated with this morning's session. I can't help but think of all the other forms of therapy I could have enjoyed instead: swimming blue lanes in the sunlight, soaking in the hot tub, or walking riverside through the valley to visit sheep grazing beside old stone walls. I could have been pruning my gnarly and numerous rose bushes, finishing the half-painted canvas of garden in my studio, reading a novel or writing one. I could have been dancing to music around my kitchen table, or sitting with legs crossed, eyes closed.

Leaving the pungent roots to brew, I drift to the large picture window framing the back garden, taking care not to make any sharp movements. I watch the flighty bustle at the bird feeder, which hangs in the kowhai tree like the skeleton of a Chinese lantern, and play the counting game. Three tiny wax-eyes surround the small pink cake of bug and berry at the centre of the large sphere. Two more are queuing on old nails in the trunk below, where their gold and silver plumage is best appreciated. Four — no five — hover impatiently in the branches above. I have no time for pets or caged animals, but I enjoy these daily visits.

The bird feeder was a celebratory purchase six weeks ago, on the day my brain calmed and cleared after four months of depression. I had hit the northern highway early, before the frost on the paddocks had thawed, finally able to concentrate on driving further than ten minutes across town. Wrapping my cold hands around strong coffee in a far-flung garden centre, I had compared the merits and popularity of several bird feeders on display outside, and declared the lantern the winner.

Until this morning, I had been feeling so well, and I'm angry that I've allowed someone — an alleged therapist no less — to rock my recovery. Ironically, it is this newly regained strength that seems to have contributed to the unexpected gaslighting in this morning's session. Having waited until I felt ready to re-open the doors to talk therapy, the psychologist couldn't see how she could help — there didn't appear to be anything wrong. I start to replay the morning in my head, utterly perplexed.

I am waiting in the hallway of the clinic, mouth dry and heart pounding, feeling exposed as people I might know come and go from other rooms. I'm focusing on a boring pot plant that is possibly fake, avoiding eye contact, and trying to centre with steady breaths. The psychologist I am here to see is in a fluster, attempting to unravel the self-imposed confusion of an apparent double booking. She wasn't expecting me, but when no one else shows up, I am finally ushered through her door.

It had seemed a good omen that she worked in my favourite heritage building in the city — an early twentieth-century grande dame known as The Savoy — and I pause to appreciate the generous space for thinking afforded by the high-stud ceiling and the large, light-filled room. Taking a seat on the deep leather sofa, I now focus on the woman settling comfortably into the armchair facing me.

Clean, black Doc Marten shoes peeking out from beneath her long tartan skirt recall my early university days. The woman can't be more than mid-forties — her mid-length, light-brown hair showing only hints of grey. Her soft, pale, unremarkable face, set off by the sea greens of a cosy woollen jumper, has calmed after our awkward start. In the flawed logic of first impressions, she looks like someone I could be comfortable spending time with.

Passing over a clipboard and pen, she asks me to complete a form for new clients — something I could have done prior to arrival, or while I was waiting in the hall. I can feel my pulse protesting over more time and money wasted. Accepting the clipboard with a forced smile, I complete the administration and the session proper begins.

She asks me how she can help today, as if I've just wandered in off the street into a shop on a whim. It feels impolite to ask if she recalls the reason I requested an appointment, or has read the psychiatric report I sent in advance, so I rehash my introductory email on the assumption I need to jog her memory. Since she shows no signs of having familiarised herself with my back story, I continue.

Calmly and concisely, I summarise my history of mental illness, recent diagnosis, and approaches to management. When I explain that I'm emotionally stable today, and hopeful that this will help to lay the foundations for ongoing discussion, she is visibly confused. It appears to her that there is nothing to talk about. This is not, she explains, how she usually works. Can't I talk to my friends?

It appears that the concept of preventative care is foreign to her. She is used to being the ambulance at the bottom of the cliff, and I'm telling her that I don't want to jump. Without an immediate, tangible problem to address, and a short-term goal to work towards, she doesn't know what to do with me. Or, as she phrases it, I wouldn't be getting value for money.

Now, it is my turn to be confused. She is describing her service as if a person in psychological distress can book an appointment at short notice, assuming that they are even capable of doing so. How could she possibly be unaware of the extent to which demand for psychotherapy has been outstripping supply in this country for years? I refrain from pointing out that she is not my first choice, and that many of her peers have closed their books.

When I share my expectation that it would be helpful to examine common patterns of behaviour and recent scenarios, with a view to improved self-management, she is unconvinced. Apparently, 30 years of bipolar depression and hypomania is not sufficient evidence that proactive psychological assistance would be of value.

As my body temperature starts to spike, I break eye contact to remove my jacket and drink from my water bottle. I take pains to arrange my face, concealing my frustration and bewilderment. I can't bring myself to speak frankly and risk breaching the boundaries of politeness. As far as I'm concerned, her online profile on the national register, which lists areas of specialisation, has been misleading. Does she know anything about bipolar?

In the uncomfortable silence, our thoughts mingle in the space between us, hovering above the rug. Intuiting my question, she admits that she has little experience with Bipolar Type II, and insensitively supposes aloud that most people go about their lives undiagnosed. When she suggests that she is not the person I am looking for, the moment to walk away could not be clearer, but instead I start to cry.

She is clearly not the expert I am seeking, but with the recent memory of debilitating depression still palpable, the thought of leaving without the promise of future support, even from someone ill-equipped, is terrifying. Now that I am showing tangible evidence of distress though, the atmosphere noticeably shifts. Temporary calm, it seems, is of no interest, but tears she can work with. Finally galvanised to assist, she offers a box of tissues, and switches her tone of rejection to resignation. She is willing to try and work together if that is still my wish. Feeling drained and desperate, I schedule another session for the following week.

As soon as I reach the bottom of the winding stairwell and step out onto the street, I know that I will never see her again. By the time I bundle myself into the car, I am overwhelmed with emotion and can barely see the road for my tears. Having exposed my most vulnerable self to an incompetent for the past hour, my last shreds of self-respect are appalled.

Arriving home, I sit stunned in the driver's seat, outraged and exhausted. I am yet to realise that this decisive defeat is a priceless gift, leaving me wide open to an alternative and genuine solution. For two years, I have bought into the generally accepted theory that Bipolar Type II is an incurable, chronic illness. I'm about to bust that myth wide open.

THE INTEGRITY CURE

The definition of a person who "has no filter" is a tendency to say exactly what one is thinking without considering the consequences. It neglects to describe what a person might otherwise filter through: people pleasing, cultural conditioning, fear, shame. Its linguistic neutrality sidesteps the associated risks of being judged unlikeable, inappropriate, foolish, emotional. It sidesteps the value of honesty, and the implications for integrity.

In my natural state, I wear my filter loose — a lightweight summer kaftan through which thoughts and emotions flow freely, a little too transparent for the comfort of some, when I'm standing in bright light. Fellow kaftan wearers find me invigorating to be around. Others, uncertain about how to express themselves, find me refreshing. For those who wear their filters close and heavily layered, wrapped tight around the waist and buttoned to the neck, I can be a shock, a threat, a disruption to the peace.

If your language veils your face and covers your ankles, my blunt honesty can be alarming at close range, even when I am demonstrating care by saying what I mean. Craving shameless authenticity in return, I encourage equal exchange even in the midst of conflict, but a fair match is an elusive and treasured thing in my culture.

Until I meet a man who specialises in filters, and validates and revitalises my natural state, I allow my kaftan to be sullied, ridiculed, and stuffed away. Sometimes this is done by others, but more often than not, by me. By caring for it so poorly, not wearing it proudly, and dressing so inconsistently, I become someone I don't recognise: someone low in self-respect with diminished integrity, someone very unwell.

When I first hear the voice of the integrity coach who will expose the root cause of my emotional dysregulation and bipolar episodes, I hear the voice of a fellow kaftan wearer, who wears his consistently, boldly, and with pride. He also sounds like the boy next door, which isn't far from the truth. Although we are living on opposite sides of the world, we grew up in the same city, around the same time. He sounds like someone who knows what it feels like to have sand between their toes.

As I listen to him speak in an online interview about powerful honesty, his familiar accent and colloquialisms have an impact of their own. Despite his international following, this isn't some unrelatable, unapproachable, self-help guru. The respectful, concise, and uncompromising way he expresses himself recalls my younger brother, to whom I have always looked up. When I see a picture of the coach later, he reminds me of my cousin. This feeling of kinship, together with our shared egalitarian culture, gives me the courage to reach out and connect.

Listening to his interview has been a game changer, but I resist the urge to gush and fawn, keeping my email brief and understated, in typically Kiwi style. He promptly responds to my letter of thanks and interest with humility and generosity, and a powerful process of unlearning and relearning how to be in the world begins.

For two intensive months, I immerse myself in his knowledge, in every format I can lay my hands on. I join the ranks of his Integrity Army community, and knuckle down for a self-prescribed, mental health boot camp. My goal is to stop worrying about the impact of my honesty on others, and focus on its essential importance for me. I read his books, and work my way through his courses. We meet online for a free, individual coaching session, during which my legs shake uncontrollably from start to finish.

The voice of the boy next door becomes the voice in my head until he efficiently equips me to free my own. I like that he is a talented writer, a musician, and a dancer. I like that he is shameless, and calls a spade a spade. I like how his wisdom, grounded in Stoic philosophy, is delivered like a chat over a beer in a pub. In his no-fuss, no-frills fashion, he steps me through how my relationship with emotions, and my communication and behaviour, has been undermining my self-worth to the point of chronic mental illness.

He is experienced in the various ways that emotional suppression can wreak havoc internally and externally. He helps me to understand the damage to integrity and relationships that can result from weak honesty, and the absence of personal boundaries. He shows me how to reframe my thinking, communicate differently, and hold myself upright in the world. He turns me inside out.

Over the course of two months, as each day of learning and practice promises and delivers new revelations and inner strength, I bank over 100 hours of life-changing knowledge and skills — the equivalent of 4 years of fortnightly therapy sessions with an effective clinical psychologist. Along the way, I laugh when he swears, gasp with light bulb moments, weep with gratitude, and share my journey with fellow students on a similar path. I joke, with all seriousness, that no one should be allowed to graduate childhood without these skills. This education is so affordable, and the benefit-cost ratio so astronomically imbalanced, that I beg to pay for my first free session, but he politely declines. He is, quite simply, happy and humbled to help.

If my belated bipolar diagnosis turned the lights on, what Dan Munro teaches me about honesty and integrity sets the room on fire. Bipolar Disorder Type II was the symptom, not the true cause of my suffering. As my ignorance, crippled mindset, and emotional crutches burn, I rise like a phoenix from the ashes. The palpable sensation of inhabiting a new mind is nothing short of radical transformation. With unprecedented clarity, I change from being someone who avoids the world beyond their front door, to someone confident in their ability to manage any situation without falling apart. I shrug off my limiting fragility, and step into the definition of resilience.

I know with absolute certainty that for me, mental illness has been the result of straying from the path of integrity paved with my values. I know it in my bones, and my stories are my proof. For 30 years, I had rewritten my code of conduct in response to the world around me, and my system had repeatedly malfunctioned. With my original settings restored, the challenge is to protect them with my life. Two months after first hearing Dan's powerful honesty, I walk away from the inevitability of mental illness, and into an exciting, alternative future.

The two-month period I spend immersed in Dan's coaching is the average expedition to summit Mount Everest, and my achievement is as exhausting as it is extraordinary. As I sit one morning, looking out on my garden, the realisation that I have reached the mountaintop is a moment of transcendence. My present is in clear focus, and the cloud cover over my future is dissipating. The snow-capped peaks that await me are slightly blinding but stunningly beautiful. I can see the steps I took to reach this place, without knowing my destination.

TUNING IN

Powerful, centralised calm has followed another chakra earthquake in my lower back. A tectonic release of energy, which I experienced after bipolar diagnosis, and coming out about mental illness, has happened again as I let it go. As the process of psychological healing comes to completion, I can feel my glorious wholeness making new space for personal growth. If "we're only as old as we feel", I am 30 years younger: at 48, I feel like my 18-year-old self. My ideas, enthusiasm, and sense of vitality are crackling like fireworks, but this time I am not compelled to rush or explode, only to blaze and light the way for others.

The process of healing, which might equally be described as learning, has revealed that I have long mistaken self-reliance for resilience. Not wanting to be a burden, I have erroneously tended to others without putting on my own oxygen mask first. I'm learning that the road to resilience goes both ways, and starting to trust that in times of change, others can provide me with valuable information, insight, and support.

Fuelled by my new-found clarity and confidence, I've taken great strides and reached a crossroads. I'm embracing a less rigid, more agile approach to life, but I'm still emotionally processing the bold direction I've chosen to take. I am slowly restoring faith in my strong intuition, which has suffered from being labelled mentally ill. Over the past three years, doubting the wisdom of every significant decision has been tiresome — an interim measure that is now surplus to requirement. You have helped me in this.

Dovetailing the man who enabled my recovery from bipolar, you have been the yin to his yang, your intermingling voices steering me inward over the course of a winter and into a spring. We had first met three years earlier, in my home overlooking a peaceful Dunedin valley. The house belonged to me that day, but was soon to become yours — a junction that would forever connect us.

The intense energy between us had been apparent as soon as I sat down to face you. I experienced your joyful female presence like sun on my skin and a resounding bell in my spirit, my brain fizzing with the magnetism of a fellow traveller. I sensed emotional warmth, powerful intelligence, generosity, curiosity. I sensed that you were important, but I didn't yet know how.

Three years after our first encounter, I recall that you are a personal consultant, and reach out for your support. Today, we tap into our psi power to contemplate my future. I've explained that I'm at a crossroads. You know where I have come from — after all, you are part of my history. You know of the deep sadness that followed our exchange of a home, and the diagnosis that followed. There is nothing more that I need to say. We tune in.

As you survey the valley from the north-facing study that I once called mine, you share a vision of a flower in my garden, one that was seemingly never going to bloom. It has suddenly opened, as if overnight. Can I see it? I describe the dusky pink winter rose beneath the tree on the south side, which has finally flowered two years after it was planted. You have sensed my recent, rapid and unexpected transformation, and, perhaps, the two-year hibernation needed to write this book.

You ask if there is a house sale and relocation on my horizon, and I quietly confirm. I share my vision of being a nomad, my desire for international travel. As you sit with this information, I silently reflect on my current state. I no longer need to belong anywhere in particular, now that I feel at home in myself. After years of being too fearful of emotional instability to travel, I can now trust in the strength of my wings. I am craving different cultures, climates, tastes and tongues. I will not be travelling "to do", but "to be". I believe that my writing, which has unlocked my past, is also the key to my future.

You agree: Dunedin is no longer serving me. You challenge where I see myself in the future: I am close, but a little too far east. This is a time in my life when I need to be grounded emotionally. I have been picturing England, but you see me in Ireland, where my tears can fall freely on the earth. You see a cottage in the country. The old bones of an ancestor are calling me from the ground. Later, when I mention this to my mother, who is tracing our family tree, she shares that she has envisaged me happy in Ireland. This is somewhere I have never been, and I open myself up to the possibility.

I have associated the abandonment of my work, home and place with mental illness, and I'm concerned that those who care about me, who have not yet fully grasped my recovery, will perceive my decision to leave as more of the same. You see a river, which could be mistaken for others I've flowed down before. It's moving in a familiar direction, but it's not the same water. You pause for emphasis, and repeat yourself: this is not the same water.

You see me shifting professional gears, and my readiness to collaborate with a man who plays an important role. You confirm my hunch: I have done everything I need to in this regard, for now. I must allow the seeds I have sown to germinate — the man needs time. You encourage me to consider myself a thought leader; this isn't complicated — all I have to do is simply and freely speak my mind.

You see me with people in Auckland before I leave New Zealand, and this will require grace and courage. I see my father, to whom I have recently extended an olive branch after three years of estrangement. Soon, a younger man from my hometown will step into the picture, who I have not seen coming. This new friendship will boost me up into an even stronger version of myself. I won't have to do this alone.

We pause our exchange to enjoy a quiet moment in the warm afternoon. You have seen everything that I see for myself and more. It's time for you to blow out the candle that has focused your energy. It's time for me to go.

———

ACKNOWLEDGMENTS

Words cannot adequately express my gratitude to Dan Munro, who changed the ending of this book and the course of my life. I am thankful also for the guiding lights who helped me reach the place where I could benefit from his coaching: Liz Moolenaar, Mental Health Clinician; Dr Rene de Monchy, Psychiatrist; Elizabeth Zizik, Nutritionist, Herbalist and Mental Health Nurse; and Kim Forrester, Wellbeing Consultant.

Once our eyes adjusted to the light, my belated diagnosis and subsequent recovery revealed the furniture my family and I had been bumping into and tripping over for so many years, in our efforts to reach for each other across a dark room. I thank them for their love and support.

I have been fortunate to have friends who are the epitome of grace under fire. Special thanks to long-serving cheerleaders Liane Koutris, Sarah Cutfield, and Balsam Al-Dabbagh for the sounding boards and pom-poms. To friend, author, and writing teacher Majella Cullinane: thanks for your encouragement on all fronts.

Many writers, past and present, informed, inspired, and kept me company as I shaped this book and climbed a mountain of change. In particular, I acknowledge Dr Kay Redfield Jamison for her books on bipolar, creativity, and exuberance; Roberts et. al for *The Bipolar II Disorder Workbook*, which connected so many dots; Professor Julia Rucklidge for *The Better Brain*, which informed my approach to treatment; and Hannah Gadsby for *Ten Steps to Nanette*, which inspired courage at my lowest ebb. Now, as Elizabeth Gilbert would say: Onward.

ABOUT THE AUTHOR

Donelle McKinley is a writer, editor and publisher. She began her professional life in the wonderful world of rare and collectable books, and moved on to roles at McGraw Hill and Otago University Press. Beyond publishing, she has worked in the digital space for the love of cultural heritage, the arts, and higher education. Donelle holds degrees in English Literature, Art History, and Information Studies, and a Diploma in Publishing. She studied Book History at New College, University of Oxford.

———

donellemckinley.com

www.ingramcontent.com/pod-product-compliance
Lightning Source LLC
Chambersburg PA
CBHW032336300426
44109CB00041B/1071